"A savvy book by a savvy writer and educator, written with clarity and wit, providing worthy insights into the diverse challenges confronting screenwriters . . . Truly a worthy new contribution to the literature."

—Prof. Richard Walter, UCLA Screenwriting Chairman

"Full of savvy advice about the screenwriting trade . . . Kouguell's humorous anecdotes from the front line are themselves well worth the price of admission. Strong on the fundamentals of craft as well as business protocol, the book left me wishing it had been available when I was just starting out in the biz."

—Will Scheffer, writer/creator/executive producer, *Big Love;* playwright/screenwriter, *Easter, In the Gloaming, The Pact*

"Susan is a one-woman encyclopedia of film industry wisdom and is simply one of the most original and exciting writers I know. *The Savvy Screenwriter* is an indispensable resource. It ought to be required reading for all screenwriters, period."

—Carl Capotorto, *Sopranos* costar, playwright/screenwriter, Chesterfield winner, three-time O'Neill Playwriting Fellow

"This much-needed book is both extremely informative and surprisingly readable."

—Ira Deutchman, president/CEO, Emerging Pictures; partner, Redeemable Features; Columbia University professor

"Practical, witty, and insightful. Kouguell explodes the minefields of getting your screenplay produced so you don't have to get burned yourself. Read this book before you write another word!"

—Thelma Adams, *US Weekly*

"*The Savvy Screenwriter* is that long-awaited beacon for navigating the complex shoals of screenwriting. This book is not only a word to the wise, it comes from the wise as well."

—Andrew Marton, critic, *The Fort Worth Star-Telegram*

"Kouguell has given it to us straight. *The Savvy Screenwriter* lays out a detailed plan. It first explains how to fine-tune your work. It then demonstrates how to promote an interest in, and ultimately sell, your script. The book is concise, well structured, objective—and a bit humbling."

—*MovieMaker Magazine*

"To filmmakers like Louis Malle or Harvey Weinstein, she needs no introduction. To working or aspiring screenwriters who may not know of her yet, she is an accomplished screenwriter and script doctor who has quite possibly written the most comprehensive new book you will read this year."

—*NewEnglandFilm.com*

"The quintessential how-to book for anyone starting off in the business of writing screenplays."

—Doug Witkins, president, Picture This! Entertainment

"Susan Kouguell has written an excellent book, which sticks to the most important and essential ingredients in the screenwriting career recipe. How does an aspiring writer find the time to actually write when wading through hundreds of screenwriting resources? The answer is easy: you become a 'savvy screenwriter.'"

—*UGO Screenwriter's Voice*

"As a professor and as a producer, *The Savvy Screenwriter* is invaluable to me. I use it in the classroom to enliven and enlighten discussions about producing and writing as well as personally and professionally to refresh my approaches to pitches, query letters, and treatments for my own productions."

—Garland Waller, Assistant Professor, College of Communication, Boston University

"The ultimate guide to writing and marketing your screenplay from a brilliant, witty and, yes—savvy—industry insider. Susan Kouguell has written a screenwriting book that's actually fun to read and perfectly clear."

—Alfred Thomas Catalfo, screenwriter, winner/finalist in twenty-one script competitions

THE SAVVY SCREENWRITER

HOW TO SELL YOUR SCREENPLAY (AND YOURSELF) WITHOUT SELLING OUT!

★ REVISED AND UPDATED ★

SUSAN KOUGUELL

ST. MARTIN'S GRIFFIN NEW YORK

 For information, address St. Martin's Press, 175 Fifth Avenue, New York, N.Y. 10010.

www.stmartins.com

Design by William Ruoto

LIBRARY OF CONGRESS CATALOGING-IN-PUBLICATION DATA

Kouguell, Susan.

The savvy screenwriter : how to sell your screenplay (and yourself) without selling out! / Susan Kouguell.

p. cm.

ISBN-13: 978-0-312-35575-3

ISBN-10: 0-312-35575-0

1. Motion picture authorship. 2. Motion picture authorship—Marketing. I. Title.

PN1996.K68 2006

808.2'3—dc22

2005033025

First published in the United States by TL Hoell Books

First St. Martin's Griffin Edition: June 2006

10 9 8 7 6 5 4 3 2 1

CONTENTS

PREFACE TO THE SECOND EDITION

EMPOWER YOURSELF

Bravo! You've completed your screenplay. Now what?

Forewarned is forearmed. You need to be ready for what lies ahead.

The Savvy Screenwriter reveals what's in store for you. It demystifies the film business and tells you what you really want and need to know . . . how to sell your screenplay and yourself without selling out.

Whether your goal is to write for independent or Hollywood films, *The Savvy Screenwriter* will help you to gain an understanding of how the industry works and what it expects from you and your screenplay. A savvy screenwriter is empowered. You must know what you're in for and what you must do if you are going to succeed in the film industry.

When I was brainstorming for a title for the first edition of *The Savvy Screenwriter,* one idea I came up with (but which was quickly shot down due to its incredible length) was:

"Everything you always wanted to know about selling your script, finding and working with agents and entertainment attorneys, writing queries and synopses, pitching, learning the psychology of story analysts and movie executives, understanding option agreements and development deals, tackling writing assignments and collaborations, learning the film lingo and resources . . . but didn't know whom to ask."

Okay, it was a really long title, but this is what I wanted this book to give you. And here I get the last word—or words.

In my years working on independent and Hollywood films, I endured a number of bumps and bruises, but through trial and error I finally figured out how things worked. *The Savvy Screenwriter* will help you navigate the maze set up by the film industry, which is filled with daunting rules, etiquette, and the secret society of film executives. If only I'd had a book like this, a book that would have empowered and guided me through this often difficult maze, I would have been able to devote more time to writing and less time to tending to my bumps and bruises. And I would have had a lot more fun learning the film industry ropes.

If I had known then what I know now. . . .

Throughout *The Savvy Screenwriter* you'll find personal anecdotes from my past. The movie scenes (presented in screenplay format) are fictionalized accounts of often sad but true events that happened to me in the film business—many of which occurred when I first started out. People's names and titles of films have often been omitted to protect my pocketbook and my career.

This second edition has been fully expanded and updated. It is filled with new, funny, and helpful personal anecdotes, as well as those provided by colleagues, seminar students, my students at Tufts University, SUNY Purchase, and Screenwriters Online, and my Su-City Pictures East's clients—all of whom generously agreed to share their stories (anonymously).

Throughout the book you'll also find more film industry updates, including information about online script registries, script competitions, and pitch festivals. I've also included samples for synopses, loglines, query letters, outlines, beat sheets, and a new chapter on treatments, as well as Act 1 of a sample treatment. In the Appendices you'll find expanded Savvy Lingo and more extensive and updated resource information. Each chapter has been expanded to further help you become a savvy screenwriter.

ACKNOWLEDGMENTS

Way back in 1999, something strange happened.

Almost simultaneously, several of my Su-City Pictures East's clients and my students from both Harvard and at the seminars I presented wanted to take me home with them. They wanted round-the-clock advice, information about screenwriting, and more—they wanted reassurance that they could survive the business of trying to sell their work. Because I had my own family to go home to, I wrote the first edition of *The Savvy Screenwriter*.

Without my students and clients, and their endless (and often surprising) questions, I don't think I would have written the first edition. And without the help of my many friends, family, and colleagues, I certainly would have never finished it. It was heartwarming that so many people helped me out as this book took shape and continued on when I wrote this second edition. I thank them all. Among all those who helped, the following deserve special praise for their assistance on the first edition and this second edition of *The Savvy Screenwriter.*

Thanks to my agent Ann Rittenberg, to my editor Sheila

Curry Oakes and editorial assistant Alyse Diamond at St. Martin's Press, Erin Vosgien, Donnaldson Brown, Amy Chartoff, Margie Wachtel, Judi Rothberg, and Bonnie Bluh. And very special thanks to Craig Lowy, Dan Brown and Blythe Brown, and Rose Ann Miller at Harvard University Press for their invaluable advice, generous support, and friendship, from the inception to completion of the first edition to today.

My personal thanks to my parents for their unwavering support and "enabling" my addiction to movies. To my late grandmother, Omi, who was very proud of the first edition and took full credit for any and all of my successes. And finally, to my daughter, Tatiana (already quite an actress and aspiring writer—and perhaps a future screenwriter), whose great sense of humor, vivid imagination, and generosity of spirit is a constant inspiration.

THE SAVVY SCREENWRITER

INTRODUCTION

You've probably heard that "everyone has a screenplay in his or her drawer," and this doesn't seem to be an exaggeration. Since 1990 when I started my screenplay and postproduction consulting company, which later became Su-City Pictures East, I've worked with more than one thousand clients, including Emmy-winning and Oscar-nominated writers and filmmakers, as well as surgeons, CEOs, journalists, food critics, salesclerks, dentists, lawyers, judges optometrists, artists, musicians, police officers, physicians, former nuns, and even a well-known dominatrix. But despite varied backgrounds, they've all had one thing in common—they wanted to get their scripts produced.

THE CLIENT COUCH

I have a couch at my Su-City Pictures East office. On occasion, clients have become so comfortable with me that they'll collapse on my couch, spill out their guts, and reveal their deep dark secrets, asking for advice not only about their scripts but also on how to survive the difficult life of a screenwriter. They treat me like a therapist, and I know from my own emotionally draining battles with the film industry that they probably need one.

Sometimes it all seems to be an exasperating test—a test of your self-esteem, your ability to accept rejection or to take criticism—and you'll need a strong stomach to ride the roller coaster of near misses. If you are ready for the ride of your life—and maybe want to avoid a real licensed-therapist's couch—then *The Savvy Screenwriter* is for you.

Understanding how the film industry works and how to navigate it may seem like an impossible task, but if you follow my step-by-step advice, you will discover the road best traveled. Or you can use this book as a map and jump to topics you are particularly interested in, since each chapter in *The Savvy Screenwriter* is self-contained. (This means that some information is repeated.)

In *The Savvy Screenwriter* you will find examples on how to write loglines, queries, synopses, outlines, beat sheets, and treatments. For purposes of this book, I created an original story idea, which I've titled *Career Dreams*. There is no script; my intention is to use *Career Dreams* solely as an example to illustrate samples to guide you through writing these various marketing tools. And I followed my own advice; *Career Dreams* is copyrighted and registered with the Writers Guild of America.

FACTS AND FAQS ABOUT THE BUSINESS OF SCREENWRITING

You have questions—and lots of them! In chapter 1, I'll answer the most commonly asked questions about the business of screenwriting. With your basic questions answered, you'll be ready to meet the industry professionals who are going to read your script.

HOW TO MAKE A STORY ANALYST LOVE YOU AND YOUR SCRIPT

Chapter 2 reveals story analysts' secrets. It shows you who they are, what they are looking for, and how to deliver a script that they will love. In chapter 3, the story analysts' coverage (story report) is explained. Here you will discover how a story analyst reads your script and learn what is included in the story report.

FINE-TUNING YOUR SCRIPT

How can you tell if your script is *really* finished and ready to be sent out? Chapter 4 offers all the essential tools and checklists for preparing your final polish.

GETTING YOUR CAREER IN GEAR

Now that your script is ready, it's time to get down to business—the film business. In chapters 5, 6, 7, and 8, you will find the elusive key to unlocking the mysterious film business door; learn all the do's and don'ts about writing a great query and a sensational synopsis; then discover how to prepare yourself and your pitch for that all-important meeting with film executives; and, finally, how to write a tantalizing treatment.

MARKETING YOURSELF AND YOUR SCRIPT

You may have a fabulous script, but it's not going to do any good if it's sitting in your desk drawer. Chapter 9 includes advice on developing a hit list of companies and agents. It gives you savvy shortcuts to networking and additional suggestions for screenplay opportunities. While you're doing all this groundwork, you need to seek representation. Chapter 10 shows you how to find an agent and, once you get one, how best to work together to sell your script and get writing assignments. If you are waiting for an agent's response or can't find an agent, there are other options. An entertainment attorney can submit your script and look out for your best interests; all of this is covered in chapter 11.

GETTING ASSIGNMENTS AND SURVIVING WITH DIGNITY

When you finally receive the attention you deserve for your screenplay, it's imperative to understand the opportunities and traps that lie ahead. Chapter 12 covers the basics of the option agreement and the development deal in language that you will understand. Because filmmaking is a collaborative process, you must know how to work with producers, directors, and actors. Chapter 13 gives you hands-on advice to help you succeed in your writing assignments and collaborations. Chapter 14 provides essential pointers for the savvy screenwriter, from insights into contracts to making the most of your screenwriting career. And, finally, chapter 15 offers some advice about the adventure you are about to embark on.

SCREENWRITING RESOURCES AND LINGO

The savvy screenwriter is well-versed in all aspects of the film industry. To keep you in the know, I've included two appendices: "Savvy Lingo" defines vital terminology and "CineFile" lists resources and organizations.

CHAPTER ONE

YOUR QUESTIONS—MY ANSWERS

Following are the questions most commonly posed by my clients, students, and seminar attendees about working in and surviving the film business.

What exactly is a spec script?

A spec script is a screenplay that is written on speculation—meaning without payment or before a deal has been negotiated.

How likely is it that I will sell my spec script?

To be honest, selling a script is like winning the lottery. Someone has to win the lottery . . . and some writers do sell their scripts! To keep sane and focused against such staggering odds, it's important to keep in mind three potential goals. You want: (1) to get your script sold; (2) to get your script produced; and (3) to have it serve as a writing sample for future work.

What are the steps to getting my spec script sold?

1. Write a great script. *(See chapter 4, "Is My Script Ready for Submission?")*

2. Write a strong query letter that will entice an executive to read your script. *(See chapter 5, "The Quest for a Winning Query Letter.")*
3. Compose a strong synopsis that demonstrates why your story is great. *(See chapter 6, "Sharpening Your Synopsis.")*
4. Write a powerful pitch that will inspire an executive to buy your idea and/or script. *(See chapter 7, "All About Pitching.")*
5. Know how to write a treatment. If a company interested in your project requests you submit one, you'll be prepared. *(See chapter 8, "The Red Carpet Treatment.")*
6. Target the production companies, studios, and talent (actors, directors, producers) that are appropriate for your script. *(See the appendix on page 257 for listings of directories.)*
7. You've heard the joke: "What's the best way to Carnegie Hall? . . . Practice, practice, practice." What's the best way to break into the film business? Network, network, network. Writing is solitary, but the film industry is all about connections. No matter where you live, you must find a way to make personal contacts with industry professionals. *(See chapter 9, "Okay, I Finally Finished My Script.")*
8. Find representation. Learn how to find agents and entertainment attorneys, and discover how they can work for and with you. *(See chapter 10, "Finding an Agent," and chapter 11, "Entertainment Attorneys.")*
9. Understand how option agreements and development deals work so you're savvy when an offer is

presented to you. *(See chapter 12, "They Like Me! They Really Like Me!")*

10. Moviemaking is all about collaboration. Whether you're working with a writing partner or as a writer-for-hire, learn the necessary tools for a successful collaboration. *(See chapter 13, "Tips on Approaching Writing Assignments and Finding Harmonious Collaboration.")*
11. Know the facts to keep you and your project protected. *(See chapter 14, "Your Screenwriting Mantras.")*

A CLIENT'S CALLING

Several years ago a client told me, "I've been calling everyone that has any remote connection to the film industry, and I'm getting to the point where I'm calling anyone who's ever seen a movie!"

His determination paid off. He won two-dozen script competitions, found a prominent agent, and two of his screenplays are in preproduction.

What exactly is the Writers Guild of America (WGA), and who can join?

The WGA is a labor union that represents approximately eleven thousand writers. Eligibility is open to those who have sold literary material to or are employed by a signatory—a company that has signed the Guild's Minimum Basic Agreement (MBA). The MBA determines how you work, your writing fee, and additional fees you receive when your work is reused on basic cable, free TV, videocassettes, DVDs, and interactive media.

Members living east of the Mississippi River belong to WGA East, and members living west of the Mississippi belong to WGA West. Every member works under the same contracts and receives the same benefits.

What type of services does the WGA provide to nonmembers?

The following is a brief overview of what the WGA provides. Contact them or look at their Web sites (www.wgaeast.org; www.wga.org) for additional services:

- **REGISTRATION.** It's imperative to register your script, treatment, and/or synopsis *before* submitting it to any agent, producer, production company, or studio in order to prevent accidental theft of material. Registering your work establishes a dated record of your material's existence and your claim to authorship. Should legal or official Guild action be taken, an employee of the WGA may produce the material as evidence.

You may register your work for a period of five years, after which time you may renew at the current registration fee. It's easy to do. You can register your script online, in person, or by snail mail. As of January 2006, the cost was $10 for WGA members in good standing and $20 for nonmembers.

Once you've registered your material, notice of registration goes on your title page as follows: REGISTERED WGAW or WGAE. (You can include the registration number, but it's not necessary.) Do not include a photocopy of the Certificate of Registration with your script. Registration with the WGA does not protect titles. Registration does not help you to become a member of the WGA.

- **AGENCY LIST.** The Guild Signatory Agents and Agencies List is available on the WGA Web site: www.wga.org.

Do I need to copyright my script and/or treatment if I have registered it with the WGA?

Yes, you must register your script with the Copyright Office *before* submitting it to any agent, producer, production company, or studio in order to establish a dated record of your material's existence and your claim to authorship. The copyright is in effect for the duration of the writer's life plus seventy years. A copyright provides additional legal protection, which WGA registration does not. As of January 2006, the registration fee was $30. *(See the appendix on page 257 for contact information.)*

Is there anything wrong with an agent who is not a WGA signatory?

There is nothing "wrong" per se with an agent who isn't signatory to the WGA. However, agents who are not signatory may charge reading, copying, and/or consulting fees. More important, nonsignatory agents do not have to abide by the WGA rules, which protect writers' interests. *(See chapter 10, "Finding an Agent.")*

I need advice on sensible ways to protect myself without becoming a paranoid freak:

- ***What's the best way to mail a script?***

Mail your script in a secure padded envelope or in a Priority Mail envelope to avoid pages being bent or ripped. You may want to send it with a Delivery Confirmation, which is less expensive than sending it certified or return receipt. Contact your local post office for more details.

- ***What's the best way to tell people about my script?***

  "Just the facts, ma'am." Give people the basics. Obviously, you don't want to give away too much because you want an executive to request your script.

- ***Is the logline the best thing to tell?***

  Yes, using your logline (a one-sentence description of your script) to pitch your screenplay is a good tool.

- ***If my script is completed, registered with the WGA, and copyrighted, can I tell anyone and everyone about it?***

  Yes, but use your best judgment. Telling everyone about your script exposes your ideas to the world, so be selective as to whom you choose to tell.

How many rewrites do I need to do before I finish my spec script?

I hear this question on a daily basis, and it's usually prefaced with, "I know you don't know the answer, but . . ."

There is no definitive answer. It depends on your own gut instincts, along with the feedback you are getting from a script consultant and/or film executive. You may be able to nail your script in a couple of drafts or it may take thirty drafts or more. The number of rewrites is not a reflection of how talented you are.

How much money can a beginning screenwriter expect to make by selling a spec script?

It depends on the market, the type of picture it is, and who's buying: a Hollywood studio, which could offer thousands of dollars or more, or an independent production company, which could pay you significantly less. Generally, first-time screenwriters are offered Writers Guild minimum for a project, which as of January 2006 was approximately $36,000 for a low-budget film ($5 million and under) or approximately $75,000 for a high-budget film (over $5 million). The days of selling a spec script for $1 million-plus seem to be numbered! (Visit the Writers Guild Web site at www.wga.org to see their Schedule of Minimums.)

What are the most common mistakes made by new screenwriters?

I address this question throughout the book in various chapters, but here's a brief overview:

- Submitting a script before it's ready. If you're tired of rewriting, this is not the time to submit your script. Get feedback from others to make sure it's the best it can be. You have one shot when you submit it. It's extremely difficult, if not impossible, to get a producer, production company, and/or agent to reread a script they've already rejected.
- Not taking the time to write strong and attention-grabbing queries, synopses, and pitches.
- Submitting a script that is not industry-standard-formatted, and/or has typos, grammatical errors, stains, missing pages, no page numbers, camera angles, or dense action paragraphs, and/or is over 120 pages long.

- Not knowing what the story is really about, which is reflected not only in your script but also in your query, logline, synopsis, and pitch.
- Submitting a script to a company and/or an agent before it's been requested. If you think you can "sneak it in," think again. It will be thrown out.
- Writing a script that's so personal that it lacks objectivity and, in turn, just isn't very compelling as a screenplay.

WRITE WHAT YOU KNOW. RIGHT? OR WRONG?

Here's an e-mail from one of my students:

Through my sessions with other screenwriters at the workshops I attend each week, one commonality among new writers is this: "Your first screenplay often has so much of *you* in it, that it's hard to let go and do the rewrite . . . to let the characters speak and act for themselves." I've now met several writers who say their first script had this problem. It's funny. We're advised to "write what you know," but if it takes on too much of you it becomes a stumbling block. So, here's my turn of the phrase advice: "Write what you know, but stay out of the show!"

Good advice. You must remain objective when writing a script based on your personal experiences.

What's a good way to choose an agent to query?

There are hundreds of agents from which to choose, so narrowing it down is exactly what you need to do. *(See chapter 10, "Finding an Agent.")*

- Read trade publications to learn who's selling scripts. Some of these publications also list agents seeking new writers to represent. *(See the appendix on page 257.)*
- Target agents who represent writers in your genre.
- Research the agents who represent screenwriters who share your writing sensibility. *(See the appendix on page 257.)*
- Attend script conferences, pitch and film festivals where agents may be speaking as panelists or listening to pitches. This gives you the opportunity to meet the agents in person and learn who may be right for you. *(See the appendix on page 257 for trade publications, which list various events.)*
- If you write low-budget, art-house-type scripts, query a literary agency rather than a packaging agency. But if, for example, you write mainstream, big-budget action scripts, targeting packaging agencies may be a better choice.
- Various online publications have message boards, which are another valuable way to share information with other screenwriters. *(See the appendix on page 257.)*

How can I protect myself from a company stealing my pitch idea?

You must register and copyright your pitch idea prior to your meeting. Bring your synopsis and/or treatment to your pitch meeting. It must include a cover page, which has the same layout as your script's cover page. This should state your name, contact information, copyright symbol (©) with the year, and your WGA registration number. After your pitch, the executive may ask for your synopsis or treatment, or you may ask if you can give it to the executive. If you pitch on the phone, follow up with a letter and the material you pitched with the cover page as noted above. Keeping a paper trail is your best defense against theft of ideas.

My script is completed, and I'm ready to start making calls to production companies to determine to whom I should address my query. I've heard that there's a slight chance that if I catch an assistant at the right moment I can pitch my script over the phone. What advice can you give me?

Bravo for following the savvy rules! Calling ahead to confirm the best person to query and to confirm the correct spelling of the person's name is exactly what you need to do. And yes, if you're lucky and the stars are aligned, you just might catch an assistant at the right moment when he or she has a few seconds to talk. Assistants are scouting new material and new talent, and like you they want to make their mark. If they discover that winning script and/or new talent, it may help to further their own careers.

Do your research before you make your call; you must know the scripts the company currently has in development and what they've produced. Personalize your call to fit the company's profile, and demonstrate that you've done your research by stating why your script may be a good match for their company. For example: "Given the XYZ films you've produced, I believe my script shares a sensibility that may be of interest to your company."

Keep in mind that if your script is too similar to films

they've already produced or scripts they have in development, you must indicate how your script is unique. You might be asked: "Tell me what your script is about." Pitch your one-sentence logline and speak slowly and clearly. *(For specific tools for writing loglines, see chapter 5, "The Quest for a Winning Query Letter.")* If you don't have a good memory, or you tend to get nervous on the phone, have your written logline in front of you. Don't just *read* it—be engaging. This is your chance to grab the assistant's attention. If the assistant is interested in hearing more about your script, you'll be asked specific questions.

Do you think submitting work to script competitions is really valuable?

Winning or placing as a finalist at a prominent screenplay competition will indeed help get your work noticed. If you win or place as a finalist, then including this information in your query letter will help put your query on the top of the pile. However, there are hundreds of script competitions, and you need to be discriminating. Entering a high-profile competition whose judges are well-known and established industry professionals, that has a cash prize, and announcements in the trades, is worth your time and money. Lesser-known competitions with no-name judges, no film industry affiliations, and no cash prizes, don't add much credibility to your work.

The Web site www.moviebytes.com has a very valuable Contest Report Card where writers post their opinions on contests. *(See chapter 9 for more details on screenplay competitions and the appendix on page 257 for more resources.)*

If I have an idea for a screenplay but haven't written it yet, should I still query companies with my idea?

Doing this is too risky. If the company is interested in your project, they will want to see your completed screenplay *now*. Having them wait for weeks, months, or longer while you're writing your brilliant script risks losing their attention. Remember, there is a revolving door of executives, and whoever's there today may be gone by the time you're ready to send your script.

Are Hollywood studios open to receiving scripts from writers who don't have agents or previous screenwriting credits?

It's very unlikely that any studio will read a script not submitted by an agent (otherwise known as an unsolicited script), especially if the writer hasn't had a script produced before. Studios are deluged with scripts on an hourly basis, and they rely on agents as a screening mechanism.

Studios must also protect themselves from being sued. A script submitted by an agent or a manager and/or an industry referral creates a more detailed paper trail, which avoids lawsuits. For example: a studio releases a film that is similar to an unsolicited script that was sent to them. The paper trail serves as proof of submission should a dispute arise.

If I don't have an agent or can't afford an entertainment attorney, do I have any options to submit my script to a producer, studio, or production company?

If you have a connection to an industry professional, sometimes a personal recommendation may help to break down the barrier. *(See chapter 9, "Okay, I Finally Finished My Script.")*

Is it worthwhile to query a star's production company if I don't have an agent?

Yes it is. The worst that can happen is that you get a "thanks but no thanks" response or no response at all. You must send an enticing query letter that illustrates how your script will be of interest to them. If you can include in your query that you have won a script competition, or that you wrote and/or directed a short film that has won a film festival, it will further demonstrate your professional credentials.

Your script must have a compelling, well-developed, and of course brilliantly written role for the star. Your script *must* be a match for the star. Research: (1) the star's previous work, (2) what the star's company currently has in development, and (3) new work that is about to be released.

Keep in mind that A-list actors are a tough challenge because they are in high demand. Having a personal referral from an industry professional who works or has worked with the star is certainly advantageous. And, of course, if your script is requested, be sure that you submit a script that is the best that it can be. *(See the appendix on page 257 for a list of resources.)*

I don't have an agent. Should I also query directors in addition to producers and production companies?

Yes. You never know if the director is seeking just what you've written. Your query must demonstrate why your script is a perfect match for the director. You must research the director's previous work and any of his or her films about to be released. As always, if your script is requested, be sure to submit your best work. *(See the appendix on page 257 for a list of resources.)*

What are managers, and do they do the same job as agents?

Like agents, managers work with writers to strategize their careers and set up pitch meetings with interested companies and talent; submit clients for writing assignments; make introductions to attorneys, publicists, and financiers; and help package projects. Agents and managers know the players: who's buying scripts and what they're buying, what's in development and production, who's looking to produce, and where the financing is.

Generally speaking, managers are known to be more career-oriented while agents are known to be more deal-oriented. Often, managers represent fewer clients than agents do, giving them more time to nurture and develop writers. Sometimes managers offer feedback on writers' work as well as guide writers in the film industry. Most managers have relationships with agencies and will send material to them.

Managers are not signatories to the WGA; they do not have to abide by the WGA rules. Many screenwriters have both agents and managers. Whether you need both an agent and a manager depends on your career strategy and/or screen credits. Here is where agents' and managers' jobs differ:

- Managers' commissions are usually 15 percent of what their clients earn, whereas WGA signatory agents can only charge 10 percent.
- Managers can produce scripts written by their clients, but agents who are signatory to the WGA cannot; however, there are some recent exceptions. (*See chapter 10, "Finding an Agent."*)

What happens after I send my query letter?

While you are anxiously waiting by the telephone and your mailbox for a reply:

1. An executive's assistant reads your query.
2. If he or she thinks that the company will be interested in your script, it will be passed on to the executive.
3. If the executive is interested, you or your agent (if you have one) will be contacted to submit your synopsis and/or spec script.
4. If the executive likes your synopsis and/or spec script, you or your agent will be contacted to set up a meeting, at which time you may be asked to pitch additional projects.

What exactly is a release form, and should I be afraid to sign on the dotted line?

A release form is a legal document that protects producers, production companies, and studios from charges of theft of ideas. For example, if the company has a similar script in development or released a film that resembles your script, you cannot take legal action against them. The release form states that you are the owner of the material and that you have the right to sell it.

If a company/studio reads your query letter and is interested in reading your script, generally it will send you a release form to sign you if you do not have agent representation. Chances are they will not read your script unless you sign the release.

If the release form is from an established and reputable producer, production company, or studio, you should not be afraid to sign on the dotted line. However, if you have *any* doubts or questions, contact an entertainment attorney to review the release form with you.

How do I know if my script is right for an independent production company or a Hollywood studio?

It generally comes down to budget, and there are some projects that can go either way. Independent production companies (also known as "indies") produce films averaging about $10 million. These films are usually character-driven stories with a small cast, a few settings, and/or little or no special effects. Studio films are now reaching almost the $200 million mark. Scripts that include a lot of action, special effects, and major stars are more geared to the studios.

My script is about a personal experience but I don't know how to categorize it for the cover page of my screenplay and for my pitch and query letter. What's the difference between: "based on a true story," "inspired by a true story," and "suggested by a true story"?

Based on a true story: Your script has no or minimal fictionalization of an actual event or events.

Inspired by a true story: Your script has substantial fictionalization of an actual event or events.

Suggested by a true story: Your script is predominately fiction, but the idea came from an actual event or events.

If I am interested in directing my script, is it worthwhile to make a short film to get attention for my work?

Absolutely. Writing, producing, and/or directing a short film can be a useful calling card. Some agents and producers are more interested in looking at a short film rather than a feature-length script. However, don't submit a short film without sending a query first.

I've received several spiffy little letters from legal departments saying they didn't read my query letter, no one touched it, and they basically returned it to me holding it in a pair of tongs and soaked in antibacterial lotion. Okay. I tried. So now it looks like I need to find an industry referral, but what exactly does "industry referral" mean? It's not the same as a letter of recommendation from a screenwriting professor, is it? Is that different from your uncle Ted knows his cousin Frida's hairdresser who happens to do Salma Hayek's hair? Is it something you'd attach to a query letter? How would an agent/company really know if your referral is legitimate?

The first issue to address is if your query letter is really doing its job. (*See chapter 5, "The Quest for a Winning Query Letter."*) It's a bit surprising that legal departments are returning queries without reading them, but the reason might be that you submitted your query to a company that specifically stated in their guidelines that they don't accept query letters.

An industry referral means that a film executive, an agent, a name director, a producer, and/or an actor has read your script, believes in it, and has offered to let you use his or her name when contacting agents and/or companies. The person who gives you the referral does not provide a letter of recommendation unless an agent and/or a company has specifically asked for it. (This rarely happens.) You would simply state in your query letter something like:

"Famous Director suggested I contact you regarding my screenplay."

An industry referral is not the same as a letter of recommendation from a screenwriting professor. Unless your screenwriting professor tells you: "Contact my colleague at Paramount Pictures, and you may use my name," stating in your query letter that your screenwriting professor thinks that you're the next William Goldman is certainly an ego boost, but it won't carry any weight. The personal connection your screenwriting professor has to the Paramount Pictures executive is a valid industry referral.

In the film industry everyone knows everyone else, and if they don't they know someone who does. So the moral of the story is: if you state in your query that Famous Director suggested you contact Famous Agency and you have not been honest, it will come back to haunt you. If agents or executives question your referral, they will contact Famous Director to see whether or not your referral is legitimate. If it isn't legitimate people will remember your name, but for the wrong reasons. You'll become Infamous Screenwriter Who Can't Be Trusted.

If you're "only" a writer, would it be useful to attend film festivals or is it best to stick to screenwriting conferences?

It's very beneficial to attend both. Screenwriting conferences are a good way to learn more about the screenwriting craft and to network with agents, executives, and other screenwriters to share information about their experiences. Film festivals are also a very valuable way to meet and develop relationships with rising new directing and producing talent. Go to the films in the genre you're working in, meet the directors and producers, and make connections. You never know if the next project they're looking for is yours.

WHAT? YOU DON'T WANT TO WATER FLOWERS?

Finding an industry-related job right out of college can be a challenge. One of my students worked as a story analyst during college for a very prominent theater company that wasn't willing to pay her more than $75 per week after she graduated. She needed to find a *real* paying job, preferably in the film industry.

Here's an e-mail she wrote to me after her graduation:

I recently had an interview at an independent movie house. They wanted me to bring two references. They told me that they were flooded with résumés and cover letters for this job, and that I should be proud of myself for making it past the first round and being called for an interview. (They interviewed me at the concession stand! My résumé and cover letter were spread out across the popcorn maker.) The job title was administrative assistant, and the ad specifically said they were looking for recent college graduates. But when I asked what the main responsibilities of the job were, the people interviewing me said, "Delivering videotapes, filing papers, and, most important, watering the flowers in the lobby." (They explained that these were expensive flowers.) As they were telling me this I was thinking, "I needed two references for a job watering flowers?" When

I asked them why they specified recent college graduates, they explained that too many people aged thirty-five and over were applying, and since they are a young twenty-something staff they would feel weird having someone older than them being their assistant. I'm surprised that someone over thirty-five would want a $10-an-hour job filing, delivering videotapes all over the city, and watering a pot of flowers sitting on top of the concession stand.

This interview really showed me how desperate people of all ages and walks of life are to get into the entertainment field, even if it means doing extreme grunt work such as this. I didn't wind up getting the job mainly because I asked, "Is there room for growth in this position?" They gave me a worried look and said, "Oh, you want a job with growth?" I thought everyone wanted a job with growth!

This led to her question:

How can a person establish themselves when they are fresh out of college without a credit or connection to his or her name?

My e-mail response went something like this: Since you're not one of the fortunate few to have a personal or family connection to executives, be prepared to start at the bottom. For example, in most agencies agents must start in the mailroom and work their way up. I went on to include additional tips to break into the film industry (see below), and I suggested she emphasize her prior position as a story analyst at the theater company on her résumé. I also encouraged her to continue sending out her résumé everywhere she was interested in working. I cheered her on, encouraging her to persevere, network, and to not get discouraged.

And what happened next is not a contrived Hollywood happy ending. During the summer, my student e-mailed me with great news. She followed my advice and was hired (for pay!) as an associate literary manager!

TIPS TO BREAK INTO THE FILM INDUSTRY

- **INTERN AT A COMPANY.** Keep your options open as to various intern positions to get your foot in the door.

- **INTERN AS A STORY ANALYST (READER) AT A COMPANY.** When they see how good you are and your commitment to their company, chances are you'll eventually be hired. If you don't get hired due to budgetary constraints, you can note your story analyst experience on your résumé, which will help you to get work at another company.

- **VOLUNTEER AT FILM FESTIVALS AND SCRIPT CONFERENCES.** Doing grunt work may be aggravating, but keep your eye on your goal: you'll learn more about the business and get the chance to meet executives.

- **WORK AS A PRODUCTION ASSISTANT (P.A.) ON STUDENT AND INDEPENDENT FILMS.** P.A. positions are usually unpaid, but this is a chance to learn more about filmmaking and the film industry, and to network with others.

- **READ THE TRADES.** Most publications list paid and unpaid job opportunities. *(See the appendix on page 257.)*

You may have to find work unrelated to the film industry as your "day job" to pay the bills, but be open to volunteering or interning at companies. Most of us have done it, and it's often slave labor. It may be humiliating to run errands for someone (with a college degree in your pocket), but this is where you can make good impressions. Demonstrating your hard work, reliability, smarts, and commitment to learning more about the business shows that you have what it takes. The key is networking and perseverance as you put your best foot forward. *(See the "Networking Know-How" section in chapter 9, page 178.)*

THE BREAK-IN

Fresh out of the Whitney Museum Independent Study Program, inspired to write and make films, I was raring to go. But I had to pay the bills. I was living in cheap sublets with strange (note the euphemism) roommates and moving every couple of months. Determined to establish myself in the film industry, I volunteered at film festivals and film companies to learn about the industry, and I interned at a studio to train as a story analyst. At night, I worked the lobster shift typesetting (that dates me) at Bloomingdale's and held an assortment of other paid work and temp jobs that were completely unrelated to the film industry. These various odd jobs (and some of them were indeed very odd, like wearing a sandwich board to advertise a gallery) provided me some schedule flexibility (so I could write and, if lucky, sleep) and a steady paycheck.

When I finally broke in and started working as a story analyst for various companies, I became friends with other readers, interns, secretaries, and assistants. Several years later, many of these same colleagues became top executives and agents, and we were able to help each other out—and our friendships continue to this day.

Is there something screenwriting students should be doing during college to make it possible for them to enter the industry once they graduate?

Take advantage of your time in school to learn your craft. Build relationships with your classmates. Work on student films. Collaborate on projects. Write as much as you can, build your portfolio, and ask professors for feedback. Use this opportunity to your best advantage. Ask your professors for advice: how did they start out, and do they have suggestions for contacts in the industry that may help you. If your schedule allows it, volunteer at screenwriting conferences, as well as film and pitch festivals, and network! *(See chapter 9, "Okay, I Finally Finished My Script.")*

How can I really succeed in the film industry without selling out?

Understanding and educating yourself about the film industry and all that it entails will give you the tools needed to make informed decisions based on your goals. Remain true to and passionate about your work.

SELLING OUT!

One of my clients, whose screenwriting career is just about to break wide open but is experiencing dizziness from the roller coaster ride and sleepless nights, told me, "I shot awake from a weird nightmare last night—I had finally gotten my big break. I was hired for millions to direct the remake of *Soylent Green*. The producers handed me the shooting script. I flipped to the end to see what the big surprise was going to be and discovered that instead of people being turned into food, they were being turned into affordable furniture by IKEA. I said, 'No problem.' And proceeded to make the film. AHHHHHHHHH!"

I can't seem to find the time to write. Maybe I'm procrastinating. Any advice?

If you think you're procrastinating, then you need to ask yourself why. Many writers are afraid of success or failure. Becoming aware of this is your first step to removing this obstacle and getting focused on your writing. Managing your time is a good way to forge ahead.

TIME MANAGEMENT TIPS

- Write down your goals. For example: "I want to write one scene per week."
- Organize your schedule. Know when your most creative and productive times are; this is the time to write. Write down your priorities and put them in order.

- Set attainable goals. If you're saying to yourself that you can write an entire act in three days, most likely this is not an attainable goal.
- Use your commute time to write or do research.
- Rid your distractions. Clear off your desk. Your writing space should not contain clutter that will get you off track.
- Screen phone calls. Tell friends and family the times when you are writing so that you're not interrupted.
- Take care of yourself. Sleeping, eating right, and exercising keeps you productive.

How do you survive having your script* almost *get produced . . . ?

Have a high tolerance level for disappointment and lots of stamina! Working in the film industry requires developing a high threshold for pain.

AGONIZING CLOSE CALLS

I have had countless close calls where producers and/or directors optioned my work and I almost had my original scripts produced . . . but didn't. There are so many variables that are out of one's control. These examples almost could be considered funny if they weren't so tragic: Private financing fell through days before shooting began; a producer for another script died during preproduction and the production shut down; a lead actor dropped out at the eleventh hour when he received a better offer, and the producers couldn't move forward without him because of a presale distribution agreement based on the star's participation. The list goes on. But sometimes it all comes together and it's okay. Films that I had lost hope for actually did get made.

Is a treatment the same as a synopsis?

Although a treatment and a synopsis are both marketing tools to sell your script or script idea, they are not the same. A treatment is a more comprehensive and detailed overview, while a synopsis is generally one page and includes only the very broad strokes of your script. *(See chapter 6, "Sharpening Your Synopsis," and chapter 8, "The Red Carpet Treatment.")*

What exactly is a treatment?

A treatment is a detailed overview of a screenplay or script idea written in prose form that is used as a marketing tool for both spec and for-hire screenwriters to sell their project. The average length of a treatment is usually between ten and thirty pages. (The executive will request a specific length.) Many writers write treatments solely for their own purposes to develop their script. *(See chapter 8, "The Red Carpet Treatment.")*

Do I need to write a treatment?

It's not really necessary to write a treatment along with your spec script unless it assists you in the writing process. Studios and/or production companies usually request treatments *after* you pitch a project idea to them. They will then tell you how many pages to make your treatment. Copyright your treatment and register it with the WGA prior to submitting it to companies for consideration. *(See chapter 8, "The Red Carpet Treatment.")*

If I have ideas for music, should I include them in my script?

You may make *suggestions* if—and only if—it's absolutely necessary to your story, but be sure to identify them as just that. Potential producers and directors don't want to be told what music should be in their movie, and they know securing music rights can be difficult and very expensive.

Here's a suggestion on formatting suggested music in your action paragraph: Suggested Music: "Help Me Find an Agent" by the Savvy Screenwriters.

Is it okay to compare my script's characters to those in movies and/or books?

I don't recommend doing this because the reader may not know the character you are referencing.

In my screenplay, should I use the names of the actual actors whom I envision in various roles?

It's best not to use actors' names. This not only reads as amateurish, but this immediately limits companies and agents' casting ideas.

When I introduce my main characters should I use both their first and last names?

Yes. Using characters' full names gives them a complete identity. It also can clue in the reader as to characters' ethnicities.

My antagonist speaks with a French accent, but I don't know if I should spell out his accent phonetically.

Use phonetic spelling only if a word or phrase you're conveying specifically needs to be pointed out. Otherwise, state in your antagonist's character description that he speaks with a French accent.

If I put a graphic design on the front cover of my script, will this spark executives' attention?

Generally, industry executives do not feel that this enhances the chances of bringing attention to your script. Many feel that this screams: "Amateur!" Executives are interested in your screenplay, not the cover art.

Do you think it's wise to write for a current trend?

Writing for a trend may not be a wise choice. Although there's always that exception, trends generally fade quickly, and your script will be yesterday's news. Unless you're psychic, second-guessing the market could be a waste of time. Remember, it takes time to write a good script, and by the time you've completed your script the trend may have passed. Also, imitating the latest box-office hit will look like the imitation it is.

Write what interests you and what you want to see in the movies using your own distinct vision and passion. Knowing your market and nailing your genre will further help your script get the attention it deserves.

I have an idea for a sequel to a blockbuster film, but is it worth the risk to write it?

Unless you are looking to use this *only* as a writing sample, it is not the worth the risk. Chances are the producers of the blockbuster film already have a sequel in development.

More important, it's highly unlikely that you would be able to obtain the rights to the material, so it's not really worth your time.

Is it a good idea to write a sequel to my own spec script?

No, it's a bad idea. Your script must be complete on its own, and it's an extreme long shot that any executive would be interested in reading a sequel to a spec script unless your original script has been optioned or produced.

Can an antagonist be something other than an actual person?

Yes. Here are some examples: a tornado, a raging ocean, a dangerous animal. Whether your antagonist is a person, animal, a force of nature, and so on, the antagonist must be consistent throughout your script.

In my script, my antagonist is an evil organization, but I'm having a difficult time making this effective because there are numerous members of this organization. Any suggestions?

Put one specific person in charge of your evil organization. This way your protagonist will have one person to directly confront.

How do you handle working with temperamental and difficult well-known talent?

Don't be a doormat! Whether you're just starting out in the industry as a writer, an intern, a production assistant on a film, and so on, don't let yourself be intimidated because you're working with famous talent. Always stand up for yourself so you're not stepped on.

THE PRIMA DONNA

I've worked with many name actors, producers, and directors either as a screenwriter, a Su-City Pictures East consultant, or an associate producer. Generally, most were great, but there were times on some projects where the talent was very *challenging* to work with.

Years ago when I worked in the casting department at Paramount Pictures, a famous teen actress was decimating a long line of hapless young male actors for the role of her love interest. After each interval of five auditions, the actress would emerge from the audition room and *demand* a snack or other *necessities,* addressing me as if I were hearing-impaired and dimwitted. Showing no reaction to her attitude, (which took enormous restraint), I politely satisfied her every demand. She would then complain to her mother about her exhaustion and boredom. After each outburst, her mother plied the young prima donna with presents—a necklace, earrings, and so on—and then gently coaxed her daughter back into the audition room.

When the auditions were completed, the film's well-known director and casting director personally complimented me on my professionalism and patience with the temperamental star. Making a good impression provided more opportunities for me at Paramount. So, in the end I was the lucky one. The actress's mother had to go home with her every day and I didn't have to. Eventually, others tired of her behavior and the young star's career took a well-publicized nosedive. And I'm still here to tell the tale.

Can you explain how a studio works?

Film studios produce, acquire, and/or distribute films. Distribution is where they really make their money. Because production and the making of a successful film are essential to distribution, studios employ an array of production executives to oversee all areas of the films they release.

Studios receive approximately five hundred script submissions per month. When a screenplay is submitted to a studio it first goes to the story department where it is processed, and then it is given to a story analyst for coverage. *(See chapter 3, "Coverage.")*

Here's a brief overview of a studio's staff, starting with the most powerful position:

Head of Production or **President of Production:** This is the top banana. He or she has the power to make the final decision to green-light a film, which means the studio has now committed to financing the project and the film will go into production.

Executive Vice President of Production: This is the second in command. This executive initiates deals and oversees projects.

Senior Vice President and Vice President of Production: These executives oversee the development and production of films. Their roles vary depending on their experience and the studio. They report to the head of production and executive vice president(s) of production.

Creative Executives: These are junior executives who assist vice presidents of production and supervise development and production. They also may read scripts, write coverage, seek writing and directing talent, and initiate casting lists.

Story Editors: They supervise the story department, which uses both staff and freelance story analysts. Their responsibilities include administration and processing, reading, and analyzing all scripts that are submitted.

Story Analysts/Readers: They read and provide story reports, also known as "coverage." *(See chapter 2, "Story Analysts," and chapter 3, "Coverage.")*

What is an online script brokerage company?

These are companies whose staff may consist of former agents, producers, and/or film executives whose backgrounds vary in degrees of experience and industry contacts. Screenwriters submit their work to these companies, which for a fee will provide coverage. *(See chapter 3, "Coverage.")* If the screenwriter wants more feedback, the company will analyze the script's marketing prospects, provide notes on how to make it more saleable, and sometimes work with the writer to polish the script. If the script receives a positive coverage from the script broker, then the writer may be referred to an agent, a producer, or the broker's own online registry.

Keep in mind they have their own reputations to uphold, so, like agents, these brokerages are filtering services and are looking for the best material.

Script brokers are not to be confused with agents. They are not signatory to the Writer's Guild, which means they can (and do) charge a fee for reading scripts, and they may ask for a percentage if the script sells.

TIPS WHEN RESEARCHING SCRIPT BROKERAGE COMPANIES

- Use common sense and trust your instincts.
- Check the brokerage's credentials. You want their staff to have extensive industry experience and contacts.
- Contact them to get references. Many brokerages' Web

sites list recommendations from their clients. Note their success stories.

- Find out how long they have been in business. (Obviously a company that has been around longer and lists screenwriters' success stories is preferable.)
- Shop around and see what the average fee is for their services.
- Prior to submitting your work to them, register your script with the WGA and copyright it. *(See the appendix on page 257.)*
- Send only your most polished work.

What exactly is an Internet script registry?

Generally, for a fee, screenwriters post a logline and/or synopsis of their script on an online database where film executives, producers, agents, and so on, subscribe to the registry. (They are referred to as "subscribers.") If a post interests them, subscribers will request your script.

Do you think posting work on online registries/databases is worthwhile?

In many ways this is a very positive venue for screenwriters, particularly if they have not had work produced or don't have agent representation. Many screenwriters with whom I spoke feel that this gives them a good opportunity to be more proactive in marketing their work and they have found limited success, while others had no results and felt they wasted their money. Some screenwriters, concerned that their ideas may be stolen, prefer to target specific agents, producers, and/or production companies directly.

While some of these registries may be useful, it all comes down to the quality of your work. If your work has been consistently rejected by agencies, script competitions, producers, or production companies, then you need to consider whether your work is up to par. Ask yourself the tough questions: Have I submitted my best work? Am I targeting the appropriate registry for my work?

As with any prospective agent, producer, or production company, one must be cautious and research companies *prior* to submitting any material.

WHAT TO DO AND WHAT TO LOOK FOR

- Use common sense and trust your instincts.
- Research the registry's credentials. Their subscribers must be experienced and established industry professionals.
- Target registries with large databases of material and active subscribers.
- For production companies, find out how long they have been in business and if they are financed or have financing.
- Contact them to get references. Many sites list recommendations from their clients. Note their success stories.
- The registry should send current information about the writers and their work in newsletters or e-mails.
- The registry should keep track of who's reading your logline and/or synopsis.
- Target registries that require the interested subscriber to e-mail you for permission to look at your sample pages or to read the entire work.
- Choose registries that frequently have new subscribers join.
- Find out how much they charge. Shop around and see what the average fee is.
- Find out how long your work will be posted. The longer it's posted, the more you're getting for your money.

- The registry should have subscribers regularly look at posted work.

ONCE YOU DECIDE ON AN ONLINE REGISTRY OR REGISTRIES

- Register your script with the WGA and copyright it *before* submission. *(See the appendix on page 257.)*
- Post only a perfect logline and/or synopsis. This is your opportunity to grab industry professionals' attention. *(See chapter 5, "The Quest for a Winning Query Letter," and chapter 6, "Sharpening Your Synopsis")*
- If subscribers request your work, research and learn their credentials prior to sending them anything.
- If your post interests a subscriber, you will be asked to submit sample script pages, a sample scene, and/or the entire script. Maintain a list of the industry professionals who have read your material.

What are tracking boards?

These are specific online sites that film professionals use to track spec screenplays and share industry information, such as coverage and trends. Log-on fees can range from $15 to $300 a month.

Tracking boards may provide screenwriters more exposure of their work and, in turn, the possibility of having their work requested by executives. However, there has been some talk about the downside of these boards. For example: (1) if a script receives a bad buzz, chances for a sale are unlikely; (2) a good script promoted by an agent who has a rival may not get the attention it deserves; and (3) executives with specific personal agendas may post favorable or unfavorable comments about a script without having read it, thereby influencing the script's sale.

Is the Internet a good resource for researching agents and companies?

There is a wealth of useful information on the Internet about new companies, agents, screenplay competitions, script conferences, pitch and film festivals, and writing opportunities. *(See the appendix on page 257.)*

Do I have to live in Los Angeles to find work as a screenwriter?

Living in Los Angeles offers more opportunities because that's the town where most deals and movies are made. However, it depends on what type of work you are seeking. For more commercial projects, living in Los Angeles is certainly advantageous, but if your work is more art-house, an L.A. address isn't a must. Given today's technology, you can really work anywhere if you are willing to travel to have meetings, which is imperative to building relationships with executives.

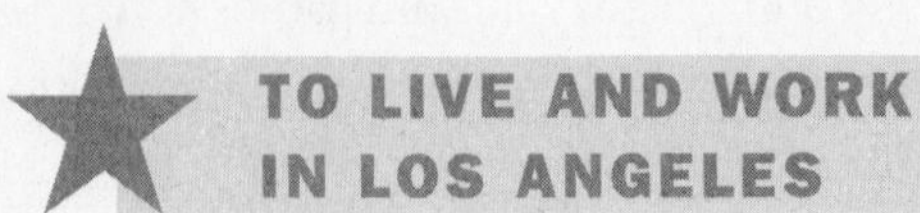

After returning from an extended trip to Los Angeles to complete a postproduction consulting job for a client, I met with Louis Malle for coffee to catch up. I told him that for the first time I was feeling somewhat torn about living in Manhattan, because it seemed that every time I went to Los Angeles I would be immediately offered very well paid work. I confided that I really didn't like being in L.A. and would always be a born-and-bred New Yorker. Louis looked me right in the eyes and said, "I know you, Susan, and your writing. If you move to Los Angeles they will eat you up. You will never write again." I heeded his advice and remained in New York, working on the projects I wanted to work on and traveling to Los Angeles for meetings and assignments. For me, and the type of projects I wanted to work on, this was the best option.

How do I find a script consultant?

The best way to find a good consultant is through word of mouth. Script consultants advertise in film magazines and teach and/or speak at screenwriting conferences and events. Contact them and ask for references. Find out what projects they've worked on, their professional backgrounds and accomplishments, and their clients' successes. Obviously, you want to choose someone with extensive industry experience and an impressive track record, but you also must feel comfortable working with the consultant—it has to be a good match for your personality and your project.

The author of this book works as a script consultant. To learn more about Su-City Pictures East's script consulting services and to read clients' testimonials visit www.su-city-pictures.com.

What should I expect from a script consultant's services?

- **HANDS-ON TOOLS:** A consultant should suggest solutions to problems with story, characters, dialogue, structure, genre, and so on.

- **OBJECTIVITY:** A good consultant will give objective feedback, letting you know what the industry expects of your script and to what degree your script meets these expectations.

- **A COMFORT ZONE:** It's imperative that you feel comfortable with a consultant and not intimidated by him or her. The consultant should provide a safe, nonthreatening environment yet be honest with you, telling you not just what you want to hear but what you need to hear.

- **INDUSTRY KNOWLEDGE:** A good consultant should have extensive experience in the film industry and know what companies are looking for and what they respond to both positively and negatively. Your goal is to have your script ready for submission; the consultant should provide the necessary feedback and tools to make sure your script is indeed ready to be sent out. Your consultant should also be able to advise you whether your script is appropriate for cable outlets or to take the independent filmmakers, or Hollywood studios, and what to expect from them.

I keep reading and hearing stories about producers, directors, and studios rewriting and often ruining screenwriters' original scripts. If this is true, why do I need to put so much effort into making my script perfect?

Yes, it's true, scripts often do get rewritten by others and the results are sometimes disastrous and often far away from the screenwriters' original intention. But don't use this as an excuse not to make your script the best it can be. Your script is your calling card. It's a reflection of your writing talent.

Eating My Words

INT. POSH MANHATTAN RESTAURANT - NIGHT

Crowded and dark Upper West Side hot spot. SUSAN, early 20s with long curly hair, enters. Her colorful hand-painted shirt and skirt are conspicuous in this ultra-trendy CROWD.

Susan, always shy and a bit on the nervous side, looks around and sees MOVIE STARLET sign an autograph for an ADORING PATRON.

Movie Starlet, 25, is an obligatory dyed blonde who behaves as if the world revolves around her. And it does. At least in this restaurant.

Susan timidly approaches Movie Starlet and extends her hand. Movie Starlet returns the gesture with a limp handshake.

MOVIE STARLET

Would you like an autograph?

SUSAN

No thanks. We've already met.

MOVIE STARLET

We have?

SUSAN

Yes. I'm the screenwriter you hired.

MOVIE STARLET

(scrutinizes Susan's outfit)

Oh yeah.

INT. POSH MANHATTAN RESTAURANT - PRIVATE DINING ROOM - LATER

Green mosaic tiled walls with matching green furnishings. TEN WAITERS in tuxes stand silent at their posts along the sole dining table in the room.

Movie Starlet eats a scrumptious dinner at one end of the long table. At the other end, Susan, with no food or drink, salivates as Movie Starlet relishes each morsel.

MOVIE STARLET

I've been thinking (takes another bite)--about my character.

SUSAN

Yes?

MOVIE STARLET

I think my character needs to miss the sixties. You know--peace rallies, bell-bottoms, gauze shirts.

SUSAN

(respectfully)

That's interesting--but your character isn't old enough to miss the sixties. She was born in 1970.

MOVIE STARLET

What's your point?

SUSAN

Well--

MOVIE STARLET

--I really think she needs to miss the sixties.

Susan clutches her forehead in defeat.

SUSAN

I think I need to get something to eat.

Movie Starlet takes another bite of her luscious meal--and takes her time to very slowly swallow and wipe her chin with her cloth napkin before she responds.

MOVIE STARLET

(sincerely naïve)

Oh. Are you hungry?

SUSAN

Well, it's nine-thirty and you had said this was going to be a dinner meeting.

MOVIE STARLET

It is. Oh! You want dinner.

Susan looks relieved as Movie Starlet signals a hovering Waiter. Movie Starlet WHISPERS in Waiter's ear.

Waiter whisks off and immediately returns with two slices of bread and a glass of water.

Susan stares at the bread and water in disbelief.

INT. MOVIE THEATER--NIGHT

SUPER: ONE YEAR LATER

A SMALL AUDIENCE is seated. Among them, Susan (in a nice thrift-store blue dress) and her friend, KATE, nervously WHISPER.

Kate, 20s, is flighty but sweet, with short-cropped pink hair and a matching pink miniskirt outfit.

The lights dim. The film begins. Susan takes a deep breath.

INSERT: SCREEN

Susan's screenwriting credit appears.

BACK TO SCENE

Susan can hardly contain her elation as Kate enthusiastically APPLAUDS.

LATER

Susan slumps in her seat and winces at the screen. Kate, with a forced smile, tries to appreciate the film.

LATER

Susan slumps even lower in her seat as she covers her eyes with her long, curly hair.

INSERT: MOVIE SCREEN

Movie Startlet, in disco outfit, overacts as she speaks directly to the camera.

MOVIE STARLET

Hey, man, even though I just told you when we were eating granola at breakfast that I was born in 1970, I still miss the groovy sixties.

BACK TO SCENE

Susan covers her ears and GROANS.

EXT. MOVIE THEATER - THAT NIGHT

A small CROWD surrounds Movie Starlet, as they take turns to congratulate her.

Off to the side, Kate comforts a distraught Susan.

SUSAN

The only things that I recognized were my characters' names. Everything was changed! That movie was horrendous! My script was butchered!

KATE

Well that's a relief. I mean, not that it was butchered--but I thought you were a better writer than that.

SUSAN

Now that's comforting.

KATE

C'mon, you still have the screenwriting credit. And you got to work with a movie star.

SUSAN

But what about my dignity?! This is the end. This is going to kill my career.

KATE

Don't be all Ms. Doom and Gloom. I bet you get great reviews.

EXT. NEW YORK CITY NEWSSTAND - DAY

Torrential rain. Susan, in yellow rain slicker, scans *Variety* and promptly pales as she reads aloud:

SUSAN

"The worst film of the decade."

THUNDER. Susan uses the *Variety* to cover her head as she runs off.

EXT. NEW YORK CITY OUTDOOR CAFÉ - DAY

SUPER: TWO WEEKS LATER

Susan, seated at a small table, drinks coffee and watches the PASSERSBY. Two filled water glasses are on the table.

Kate, now with purple hair and a matching purple outfit, runs up to Susan's table and grabs a seat.

KATE

I got here as soon as I could. What's going on?

SUSAN

You'll never believe this. Last week I got a call from an agent who requested my original script for the (sarcastic) *groovy* film? He read it!

KATE

Even after all those bad film reviews? Wow! Sorry.

Embarrassed, Kate buries her head on the table.

SUSAN

No need to apologize. (beat) He wants to represent me!!!

Kate's head pops up.

KATE

Vindication!

Susan and Kate raise their water glasses in a toast.

CHAPTER TWO

STORY ANALYSTS: WHO ARE THEY AND WHAT ARE THEY LOOKING FOR?

WHO ARE THEY?

Many story analysts (also called "readers") are recent college graduates looking to break into the film industry. Many have degrees in literature or film. They are educated, smart, overworked, and underpaid. Many are aspiring screenwriters themselves who are reading for a company to pay their bills, while others hope to work in development or other film industry positions and are paying their dues while getting a foot in the door.

Story Analysts Are the Lowest People on the Film Industry Totem Pole, but They Are Also the Most Important to You

Despite their dismal pay and low status, story analysts have a huge responsibility—to find that winning property and new writing talent! Story analysts may get three scripts to read overnight after a full day of reading. It's your job to grab their attention and make them want to forward your script to their bosses, who have the power to get your movie made. *(See chapter 3, "Coverage.")*

WHAT ARE THEY LOOKING FOR?

Understanding what story analysts are looking for will help you to deliver a script that they can champion to their bosses. They are looking for a great script, which is discussed in more detail in the next few pages, and they are looking for writing talent.

Story analysts may read a script and love the writing but still reject it because it's not the type of project their company is looking to produce at that time. However, they will file it as a sample of your writing. This sample could get you work on a project the company may have in development or on a future assignment. Or the production company, studio, or agency may contact you to see your other scripts.

I'm Tired of Rewriting, so I'm Just Going to Submit My Script Now

If you are saying this to yourself—beware! I hear this line constantly repeated by my clients and students. I've also felt this way, but I have managed to muster up my self-control and put my script away for a few days or weeks until I'm ready to get back to rewriting.

If you don't feel your script is ready, then the story analyst won't either. Story analysts read countless scripts per week, so your script must wow them.

The Weigh-In

Sounds like a boxing match, but it isn't. The first thing story analysts do is to balance your script on the palm of their hands. If it feels like it weighs more than 120 pages, story analysts will be predisposed not to like it. Why? It means more work for them, and they know from experience that lengthy scripts are rarely good scripts.

Your Goal Is to Have the Story Analyst Love Your Script

Story analysts want to like what they read. They all want to find that great script and the next hot talent. Take your time. You do not want to cause any unnecessary stumbling blocks, so do your best work before submitting it. Remember, the competition is brutal!

STORY ANALYSTS' COMPLAINTS, OBSERVATIONS, AND CONFESSIONS

During my time as a story analyst for Miramax Films, Punch Productions (Dustin Hoffman's production company), and Viacom, I became friends with other story analysts. We spent our few free minutes griping to one another, bemoaning our fate. We groaned about the often awful scripts we were assigned. We growled over the fact that screenwriters with little or no talent managed to get representation or had strong enough industry connections that allowed their scripts entrance to our company and into our hands. And then we griped some more about how little money we were earning for being tortured by bad scripts.

During this time, I was asked to write an article for a screenwriting magazine about the problems story analysts and development executives found in the scripts they were assigned. (It was an easy article to write, since those I interviewed were more than happy to kvetch!) The following is a compilation of my research, as well as my own firsthand experience as a Su-City Pictures East Screenplay Doctor and a former story analyst.

Your First Ten Pages

If your first ten pages don't grab our attention, it will be difficult if not impossible to redeem yourself later. Beware! We could stop reading your script right then and there. *(See chapter 4 for more details about the first ten pages.)*

- Clearly convey what your story is about as well as the script's genre. Don't think you're being clever by keeping us guessing. We're actually going to be guessing that you really don't know what your script is about and are confused about the genre.
- Well-paced openings will hold our attention. (This doesn't mean that you shouldn't be true to your story and rush through scenes.) Also, using long montages in your opening may risk losing us.
- Avoid extraneous scenes when setting up your protagonist. This is a common mistake that we see all too often.

Act 1

Your script must have a solid Act 1; otherwise, you're demonstrating to us that you don't know your craft. Act 1 must include the following:

- A strong hook.
- The introduction of your captivating protagonist and goals; he or she is someone we must be rooting for.
- The establishment of your riveting antagonist. However, be true to your story: while many scripts don't reveal the actual antagonist until after Act 1, the antagonist's agenda must be made clear so we understand the conflict and obstacles your protagonist must overcome and what's at stake in your story.

- An introduction of the central conflict for your protagonist.
- The setting up of what's at stake for your protagonist.
- The establishment of your subplots and minor characters.
- A plausible, unique, and fascinating story that prompts us to turn the page.
- Good pacing.
- A logical sequence of events.
- Intriguing yet well-paced setups.
- A strong turning point at the end of the act that must propel the story forward to Act 2.

Act 2

This is a tough act to follow . . . and write! Writers often use filler and/or go off on tangents to add to their page count, so know that we're onto you.

Continue to:

- raise the stakes in your story;
- put obstacles in your protagonist's path;
- further reveal your antagonist's intentions;
- surprise us with unexpected twists and turns, and intriguing revelations;
- develop subplots, which help to inform and push your main plot forward;
- build to a clear and poignant turning point at the end of Act 2, leading us to your climax in Act 3.

Act 3

This final act and particularly your last ten pages must deliver. Don't just end your script because you don't where to end your story. Starting with Act 1, scene 1, each scene should build to a satisfying climax where we are rooting for your protagonist to finally succeed.

- Keep the tone of this act consistent with the rest of your script.
- We balk at endings that are contrived, implausible, ambiguous, and haven't paid off your setups.
- The stakes must continue to rise in this act, leading to the final confrontation between the protagonist and antagonist in the climax.
- The major conflict and your subplot(s) must be resolved.
- Your protagonist must learn something by the end; this can be something your protagonist uses to resolve the main conflict.
- Your antagonist (if this serves your story) must face consequences for his or her actions.
- Your brief denouement should show us that your protagonist has reached his or her goal.
- Avoid introducing new and important characters in this act unless it's critical to your story.
- If your script opened with a voice-over, then generally it should conclude with one.
- If it's not true to your story, don't write the Hollywood happy ending. And whatever you do, don't write at the very end of your script: "You'll have to wait for the sequel to find out what happens." (You'd be surprised—I've read several scripts that have ended this way!)

Your Characters

- If you don't include character descriptions (approximate age, the character's look, and personality trait), we can't visualize your characters. (For example: Max, 30, handsome in his tuxedo and tennis sneakers, is obnoxious and sly.) We must have a visual picture, or else your characters are going to blend together.

- We want to see characters who are unique, have distinctive and surprising personalities, have clear attitudes toward each other, and serve a purpose in the story; otherwise, you are truly frustrating us. There's nothing worse than a clichéd character whom we've seen thousands of times before or characters who are interchangeable and don't have specific goals.
- We must understand what motivates characters' actions and their dialogue.
- Characters with implausible and inconsistent motivations show us that you don't have a clear handle on your characters.
- We want to see characters have clear and consistent goals, otherwise we know that you don't understand who your characters really are or their objectives in your story.
- We want to see compelling and fully developed antagonists. Like your protagonist, we want to know what's at stake for them if they succeed or don't succeed. A one-dimensional, cartoonlike, or predictable antagonist shows your writing weakness and lack of imagination.
- We don't want to read that your character is good at her job; we want to *see* her being good at her job. So, do *your* job and write it well.
- We need to see that your characters are listening to each other and responding (or not responding) accordingly.
- Using characters' names that begin with the same letter or sound the same will confuse us (unless this is a specific story choice).

• We want to see characters display their emotions, but you must be clear and consistent when conveying your characters' emotional arcs.

Your Dialogue

• A moment of silence, please. When appropriate, characters may need to pause during their dialogue stanzas to make a point. Don't overdo it, but use silences to your advantage to further capture the mood or tension in a scene.

• Know when and how to use on-the-nose dialogue. In real life and in screenplays, we know that people often don't express exactly what they're thinking. For example: David is shy and likes the new girl in school. Instead of David saying to the new girl, "I like you," which is not only on the nose but inconsistent to his shy character, he could say, "Maybe I can show you where the bookstore is after class."

While it might not ring true for characters who are manipulative, neurotic, deceitful, and so on, using on-the-nose dialogue for other characters could signal a critical change in their behavior.

There are times when it's appropriate for characters to say what's on their mind and say what they mean. For example, in the film *Being There* (directed by Hal Ashby, screenplay by Jerzy Kosinski and Robert C. Jones), Chance/Chauncey is a simpleton who speaks in garden parables that are mistaken for poignant metaphors.

• Don't detail in your dialogue what characters are reading on their menus unless it's critical to your story. This makes us hungry but, more important, it's unnecessary. You'd be surprised how many writers get stuck on such irrelevant details like menus, newspapers, books, and so on, that don't inform us about the story or characters.

- We want characters' dialogue to be distinctive and have a unique style, tone, and language. There's nothing worse than wooden and stilted dialogue. In real life people don't always speak in formal, complete sentences with perfect grammar. Using contractions, colloquialisms, slang, and so on, helps to further define characters' voices. Characters who share a long friendship, for example, can speak in verbal shorthand.
- Characters who repeat each other's dialogue unnecessarily are redundant and slow down the pacing. Certainly we know there are exceptions, and using repetition can be true to your characters and story, but too often writers make this mistake. For example: Max says, "It's cold out." Lydia replies, "Yes, it's cold out." Rather than just hearing them talk about it, let's see that they're cold. Max can jump in place to keep warm and Lydia can wrap a scarf around her neck.
- Characters can gesture their greetings like hello and good-bye. We don't have to hear them say every word; it slows down the pacing.

Your Action Paragraphs

Action paragraphs should briefly and succinctly describe what is seen on screen. For each scene, briefly describe the setting and atmosphere. For example: A dimly lit, dingy, and smoky bar. In each scene, always include *all* the characters who are seen (not just the characters' dialogue) and their actions. Action paragraphs are sometimes referred to as "directive paragraphs" or "directorial paragraphs."

- A script is not a novel. Dense action paragraphs filled with descriptions are a turnoff. Each separate action should be a new paragraph. Be brief and concise. Make each word count.

Since we are often tired and overworked, these paragraphs become a blur of black lines, and consequently we may overlook important details.

- Don't telegraph what is about to be seen and/or heard in the dialogue and/or action. For example, a bad action paragraph would state: "Tara will soon find out that her boyfriend will ask her to marry her." Let's see and hear the action unfold instead.
- Characters need to be active. In real life, people rarely just stand there (a common phrase many writers use)—they move around, chew gum, look in various directions, tap their feet, play with their hair, and so on. They don't always just enter a room, they can dash in, shuffle in, creep in, and more.
- Don't tell us the character's history. We need to see it or hear about it; otherwise, the audience won't know this information. For example, don't write in your action paragraph: "When John was ten he stuttered at the spelling bee, and since then he has always been shy speaking in public."
- Don't include characters' inner thoughts. For example, "Tara wonders if her boyfriend is going to propose to her." Ask yourself: How will the audience know what she's thinking?
- Don't editorialize. For example: "Tara is frustrated because she's been waiting twelve years for her commitment-phobic boyfriend to propose marriage, and if he doesn't propose soon she will break up with him." (This is also a badly written run-on sentence, which you must never do!)
- Each new location must have a new scene heading. If your character moves from inside his house to outside his house, this is a new scene. If you don't do this, it's evident you don't know how to write a properly formatted screenplay.

- If you don't briefly describe the setting and the action underneath each scene heading, then we're not going to be able to visualize each scene.

Your Story

- We are intelligent, but few of us have psychic abilities. If it's not on the page, we have no way of knowing what's in your head and what you intended. For example, if your characters are divorced when the story opens and this is an integral part of the plot, then establish this up front. Don't keep us guessing unless you intend to reveal this information as a surprise.
- Don't throw in the kitchen sink. Don't confuse us with extraneous characters, endless setups, and plots that don't go anywhere or have no payoff. This is a sign that you are not confident about your story.
- Don't have your central conflict drop in and out of the story; it must be consistently present throughout your script. If we see that your central conflict is doing a disappearing act, your script will disappear into obscurity.
- We may not have gone to medical or law school, but generally we are well read or have personal experience with the subject matter. We will immediately recognize if the terminology or research in your script is weak or implausible. For example, a character has a prominent scar on his back from having had his gall bladder removed. I have a prominent scar on my stomach, so I knew this was incorrect when I read it in a script months after having my gall bladder removed!
- Most of us are pretty smart and educated readers, but when using highly technical terminology make sure that it's not inaccessible or confusing. You don't want to lose us because

we don't understand the terminology. Readers and audiences don't want to feel dumb!

- Even superheroes' actions need to be plausible! If you have action scenes, be sure that they are realistic and well executed; otherwise, we will be inclined to reject your script. For example, if your superhero is piloting a plane without fuel but is in flight for twenty-four hours, we will catch this mistake!
- Don't rely on clever gimmicks if they don't have a payoff in your story. You're setting us up for a big disappointment.
- If your script jumps forward in time, make sure the reader jumps with you. Whether it's several months or several years, the time frame must be clearly indicated in your script.

Your Structure

- A weak structure signifies a weak screenwriter. You must have a solid three-act structure. Your well-paced script must have a unique and solid hook, an interesting inciting incident, a gripping and plausible central conflict, a logical scene progression, strong turning points, and a plausible and satisfying climax and resolution.
- Watch out for rambling scenes! Generally, one script page equals one minute of screen time. You must keep this in mind if your scenes run long, since we are looking for a well-paced screenplay.

Your Voice-overs and Flashbacks

- When we read voice-overs, we often panic! We don't want to be spoon-fed information. We don't want to hear the same information in voice-over that will soon be revealed in dialogue, visuals, or action. If you use voice-overs, we will dissect each word to see if it's needed or is being used as a lazy device.

- When we read flashbacks, our alarms start to go off! Generally, we frown upon flashbacks because we know flashbacks rarely work on film; they take us out of the story, slow down the pacing, and are often used as a cheap device to convey backstory that otherwise can be told in the present. If you really feel that you need to use them, know that we will be scrutinizing them to see if they are indeed necessary.

More Complaints

- Film, unlike plays or novels, is a visual medium. Endless dialogue and highly detailed description demonstrates to us that you are an inexperienced screenwriter.
- When using familiar characters and settings, you must have a distinct take and point of view or else we're going to lose interest fast. For example, if your story is about struggling screenwriters in Hollywood, we want to see your surprising and distinct spin on this.
- If you're writing a period piece or a story set in the future, specify the year and give us a clear description of the setting; otherwise we won't be able to step into the world you've created and take the journey with you.
- Avoid heavy-handed exposition at all costs. Don't over-explain information from the backstory in dialogue. We know if you're setting up a whole scene just to get exposition across. For example, don't create a scene just to explain that a character has a fear of flying because he was once an air traffic controller. This information can be simply learned in a line or two of dialogue and/or visuals.
- Don't directly address the reader in your script. We've all read at least one script—if not countless scripts—where

the writer states something like: "Reader, you're going to love this—you're in for the ride of your life now!" Actually the writer is in for the ride of his or her life—right to Rejection City if we read this.

- If it smells like a rat, it probably is one—but we don't know what something smells like unless we hear it in dialogue and/or see your character's reaction to the smell.
- Don't rely on or overuse character's facial expressions to convey ideas.
- Avoid using *your* name for one of your characters. It's distracting because we then believe this story is autobiographical whether it is or not, and it can take us out of your screenplay.
- Use a consistent name for your character or we're going to think you're referring to a new character. For example, if your character is a mother and her name is Eva, use Eva instead of Mother in your character headings and action paragraphs.

Your Audience

- You must have an understanding of your audience. For example, if your script is geared to a young audience, the children's dialogue must ring true and the subject matter must be age-appropriate. Don't condescend. Kids are smart!

Your Genre

- Know the genre of your story and stick to it throughout your script. Multi or inconsistent genres confirms to us that you really don't know what your story is about and that you don't know how to write a good screenplay.

There are numerous genres (*see chapter 4, "Is My Script Ready for Submission?")* with countless pitfalls screenwriters trip on in their scripts. The following is a brief list of the most popular genres along with observations and advice on making sure your genre delivers:

- **ACTION:** We want to take the leap off the building with your heroic protagonist, so make this leap of faith (story and actions) plausible. Whether your protagonist is an everyman or larger than life, your character must have elements we can relate to.

- **BIOGRAPHY:** We want to learn about the person's life you are portraying. Don't make assumptions that we know anything about the person or the era. Show us something unique and distinctive about the subject matter. If your script is set in another time period, then give us a clear understanding of the era.

- **COMEDY:** We want to laugh. You'd be surprised how many comedies we've read that just aren't funny. Hilarious one-liners, funny jokes, slapstick moments, and witty gimmicks may make a good stand-up routine for a comedian, but you must have a good, solid story and empathetic characters we can root for.

- **DRAMA:** We want to see your protagonist at his or her crisis point eventually resolve a compelling conflict. We want characters with whom we can relate, who are well developed, and whose journeys are unique. We want a distinguishing spin on familiar and/or identifiable issues and challenges your characters must face and overcome.

- **HORROR:** We want to be scared because you've created a frightening story, rather than scream in horror because you're a bad writer. Don't imitate other horror films. Show us something we haven't seen a thousand times before. We need to identify with your protagonist and take the journey with him or her into mysterious and unfamiliar locations—and fear for our lives! It's all about the fear of the unknown with rising stakes, not just a predictable stake being lunged into your protagonist's heart.

- **ROMANTIC COMEDY:** We must root for your protagonist to find his or her love, and we need to see how he or she will benefit from this romance. Invent clever obstacles that force your love interests apart and find innovative ways to reunite them.

- **SUSPENSE/THRILLER:** We must sense the imminent danger. Your protagonist must be in jeopardy and eventually outwit the antagonist. We want to feel empathy for your protagonist and root for him or her to survive. We don't want to read an implausible story, so research your subject matter and speak with professionals who are experts in the field you are writing about, such as detectives, physicians, and attorneys.

Your Format

- An incorrect script format shows us that you are inexperienced. Don't cheat and use a smaller font or change the margins. We will catch this immediately. Respect the time of the person reading your script.
- Never *direct* your script with camera angles. Using camera directions is absolutely frowned upon. We know that directors and producers do not want to be told how to shoot their movie!

- Don't overuse exclamation points, italics, commas, dashes, ellipses, and so on. Use punctuation strategically; otherwise you'll take—us out of . . . *your* script!!!
- Don't submit your script unless it looks perfect! No typos. (Don't rely on spell-checker.) No coffee stains. No photocopying lines. No missing or extra blank pages within the script. Believe me, you don't want us to become irritated because we are attempting to decipher text between the spots and smudges, and trying to figure out which page belongs where.

(For additional tips see chapter 4, "Is My Script Ready for Submission?")

Overnight Scripts

When I was a story analyst for Miramax, I once had six scripts to read overnight. (Why the rush? When production companies and/or studios receive a script from an agent about which there is a buzz—meaning it's hot—development executives want to be the first at the gate to make an offer to option the script if they are interested in producing it.) Clearly I was under pressure to meet my deadline, and I was exhausted. Being a responsive screenwriter, I felt an obligation to give each script a good read. But little annoyances like typos and poor formatting would send me into a tailspin and urge me to reject a script.

Think about me and my exhausted state when you submit a sloppy script. Will I want to eagerly turn every page at two A.M., or will I want to toss it aside and get some much-needed sleep?

CHAPTER THREE

COVERAGE

WHAT IS COVERAGE?

Story analysts don't just read a script and say yes or no to their superiors—they write a story report known as coverage. Story analysts read and evaluate scripts to decide whether or not the script or screenwriter will be of interest to the company or, if the script is submitted to an agent, if it should be considered for representation.

Most scripts submitted to producers, production companies, and studios by agents, attorneys, or an established industry insider will get coverage. In many cases, only the coverage, not the script, is used by executives to determine if a script is right for their company.

Coverage has a specific format. Here's an example. On the top of the first page it reads:

TITLE: Career Dreams	SUBMITTED BY: Amy Agent
AUTHOR: Susan Savvy	SUBMITTED TO: Pam Producer
FORM/PAGES: Script/110	DATE RECEIVED: 3-25-2006
DRAFT/DATE: Final/3-17-2006	READER: Alan Analyst
GENRE: Drama	LOCALE: Manhattan
CIRCA: Present Day	BUDGET: Medium

A logline, synopsis, evaluation, and rating box follow. Below are the definitions of each term:

- **Logline:** A one-sentence description of your script.
- **Synopsis:** One to two pages summarizing your story.
- **Evaluation:** A one- to two-page critique of your script that includes: whether your script is appropriate for the company; an assessment of your competence as the writer; the strengths and weaknesses of characters, story, structure, and dialogue; and an appraisal of the execution, originality, and overall strength of the story.

COVERAGE CHECKLIST

The checklist below is the last page of a coverage, but the first page that an executive reads. (Coverage is usually confidential, and it's rare that you will receive a copy.) Your goal is to have every box checked EXCELLENT.

RATING	EXCELLENT	GOOD	FAIR	POOR
DIALOGUE	√			
STRUCTURE	√			
PACING	√			
STORY	√			
CHARACTERS	√			
VISUALS	√			

The following items are also checked:

COMMERCIAL POTENTIAL: Strong: ___ Average: ___ Weak: ___
AUDIENCE APPEAL: Mainstream: ___ Youth: ___ Art-house: ___
RECOMMENDATION: READ: ___ CONSIDER: ___ PASS: ___

DEFINITION OF TERMS FOR RECOMMENDATION

- **READ:** Your script has been recommended and will be given to the development executive, who will then consider the project for production or as a writing sample for future work within the company.

- **CONSIDER:** Your script has been recommended, albeit with some hesitation, and is given to the development executive, who may or may not consider the project for production or as a writing sample for future work within the company.

- **PASS:** The company has rejected your script. No one else in the company will read your script.

A STORY ANALYST HAS CHECKED "READ" . . .

When a story analyst checks READ on his or her coverage of your script, you've passed the first test. But this is only the first step.

WHAT HAPPENS NEXT?

Development and production executives employ a varied slate of story analysts with a wide range of tastes and preferences. Likewise, the executives have affinities for different genres, but they are looking for an unbiased view of a project.

Each studio has its own procedure for determining the fate of your script. Following are two examples of how your script may travel through the ranks from a story analyst to an executive at a major studio:

1. Once a story analyst checks the READ box on his or her coverage, the script will get a second read, often by someone (like the story editor or head of development) who selects potential material for the company to produce. If that person decides your script is worth pursuing for production and distribution (as opposed to just being held as a writing sample), it will be given to several other executives for a weekend read. Every weekend, these executives will read the script and meet on Monday to share their opinions of it. If the script is of interest

to the studio, they will contact the writer or the writer's agent and a deal will be made.

2. If, for example, your script is submitted to a New York studio office and a story analyst writes an emphatic READ on a script, everyone in the story department will read it. If *they* love it, it will be passed on to a story editor, and (with luck) your great script will finally make its way to the executives. If everyone in the New York office loves the script, it will be sent to Los Angeles and the process repeats, often starting at the beginning with another story analyst.

CHAPTER FOUR

IS MY SCRIPT READY FOR SUBMISSION?

Now that you know what story analysts are looking for, you're ready to submit your script. Or are you?

AM I THERE YET?

If you are asking yourself this question because you are having doubts about your script, then most likely you are *not* there yet.

Your Script Is Your Calling Card for the Future

If you feel that a producer, production company, or studio will buy your idea and fix it, do a rewrite. If a company loves your story or idea but dislikes your writing, you'll probably be pushed off the project and replaced by another writer. Companies do not want to have to pay for rewrites. Remember, your goal is to be the only writer of your project and to receive screen credit.

Yes, Bad Movies Get Made, But . . .

You are leaving the movie theater and you are stunned. You can't believe how stale the popcorn was, but even more unbelievable was how bad the film was. You ask yourself, "How on earth did this movie get made?!" There could be countless reasons . . . from too many producers attached to a project with no one in charge . . . a weak script that producers incorrectly thought could be fixed during the shoot . . . unrealistic studio release deadlines . . . inexperienced financiers dictating the shoot. The list is endless, but the fact that bad movies do get made should not be your excuse for submitting a script that isn't the best it can be.

Get a Second Opinion, and a Third

When seeking feedback, give your script to several people who have knowledge about the film industry and will be honest. Face the tough critique now; otherwise the chances of having your script rejected by an agent, producer, production company, and/or studio are greatly increased. If you are repeatedly hearing the same comments from various sources, it's likely that their criticisms are valid. Listen carefully, and be open to suggestions. This is not the time to be on the defensive. This may be easy to say, but it's hard to do, especially if you have airplane tickets in one hand for your pitch meetings and your weak script in your other hand.

THE TOUGH QUESTIONS TO ASK A COLLEAGUE OR INDUSTRY PRO ABOUT YOUR SCRIPT

- Would you recommend that this script be made into a movie?
- Would you see it in the theater or wait for it to come out on DVD?
- How would you describe the story?
- How would you define the genre? (For example: Is it a romantic comedy or black comedy?)

- Were the genre conventions followed throughout the script?
- Are the characters empathetic?
- What were the main characters' conflicts? Were they resolved in a satisfying way?
- Did the story interest you? Why or why not?
- What were the strengths and weaknesses of the script?
- Were there any holes in the story?
- What surprised you about the script?
- Does each scene push the story forward and build to a satisfying climax?
- Were the stakes raised as the script progressed from scene to scene?
- What were the most and least memorable scenes?
- Were there any irrelevant, puzzling, and/or clichéd scenes?
- Were you bored at any point in the script?

PREPARING FOR YOUR FINAL REWRITE/POLISH

Now that you have feedback on your script, you're ready to do your final rewrite/polish.

SELF-INDULGENCE

I refer to this rewriting/polish process as my time to self-indulge. I buy a new CD. I watch films day and night, read published sicripts, and reread my favorite novels. I sit at restaurants and eavesdrop on conversations, listening for dialogue and stories. I tack up new and inspiring photos or postcards on my corkboard. I even try to take naps so I can dream about my characters. Self-indulgence is a good thing! It gets me back into the spirit of writing in a fresh and relaxed manner.

TIPS

- Set up your workstation so you're very comfortable.
- Don't feel guilty *just* thinking about your script. This is part of the writing process.
- Read other published scripts.
- See films in the genre that you're working in. This will help you to determine if your script is consistent with the genre's conventions and what the audience's expectations will be.
- Set attainable goals. Give yourself realistic deadlines for completing your rewrite. For example: Writing twenty—or even five—pages a day may be impossible for you to do and could lead to writer's block. Remember, you don't want to rush through a rewrite or create unnecessary stumbling blocks for yourself.

PAYBACK

One of my students told me that sometimes she needs help keeping to her writing schedule. She said, "I asked my obnoxious ex-boyfriend for a favor. I told him that I would pay him twenty dollars for every week I didn't write. I knew he was such a jerk that he'd hold me to it and demand the money. So far, it's working. The truth is—it's working because I loathe him so much I'd hate to pay him one cent!"

OUTLINES: SILHOUETTING YOUR SCRIPT

Outlines are helpful when fleshing out your first draft, but they should also be done with each major rewrite. Because your story and characters will be evolving with each rewrite, so will your outline.

An outline is the bare bones of your treatment or screenplay. It follows your protagonist's journey from beginning to end in sequential order of your plot. There's no dialogue, no scene headings, and no action paragraphs.

Outline Exercise on Index Cards

Think of yourself as a film editor. Here is your chance to step back and see if your script is working. This exercise will enable you to: (1) restructure your script by rearranging and/or cutting scenes; (2) determine if your characters' arcs are working; and (3) see if you've paid off your setups. (*See the section "Your Outline Must Answer the Following Major Questions" below.*)

Working with index cards may prove to be the most helpful. Using one index card per scene:

1. number your scenes;
2. write one-liners describing the main action of each scene;
3. indicate which characters are in each scene;
4. put the cards on the wall, corkboard, or floor so you can move scenes around or remove scenes.

SEPARATION ANXIETY

I confess. I used to suffer from separation anxiety. This phobia initially reared its ugly head when I was working on my first spec script. I knew that my script needed to be trimmed and restructured, but I just couldn't get myself to do it. I was too attached to my beloved scenes. I kept hoping against hope that I could get away with keeping them in. But I knew I was fooling myself. The time had come to take action.

I wrote my script outline on index cards. When I was done, I placed all the cards on a corkboard. I was then able to objectively see the scenes that were not really enhancing the story or characters in any way. I then took my next brave step: I removed these scenes and placed them in a folder with the hope that I might be able to use them later on for another script. I learned to feel good about letting go!

WRITING YOUR OUTLINE

Some companies will request you write an outline in order for them to determine if and how your story is working before they make a commitment to have you write or rewrite the script. Whether you do this for yourself or for a company, you should follow the guidelines below.

YOUR OUTLINE MUST ANSWER THE FOLLOWING MAJOR QUESTIONS

- Is my three-act structure solid?
- Are the turning points working?

- Are there places where my scenes drag?
- Are my scenes in the right place?
- Is each scene pushing the story forward?
- Is my central conflict clear?
- Are the stakes continuing to rise throughout the script?
- Are all my character arcs solid?
- Is my protagonist's journey clear?
- Are there enough obstacles for my protagonist to overcome?
- Is my antagonist's journey clear?
- Are all my story arcs clear?
- Have I paid off my setups? For example: Your protagonist discovers a secret trunk. This discovery sets up the audience's expectation to learn why the secret trunk is significant so you must include a payoff later on in your story.
- Is the subplot overpowering the main plot?
- Are my scenes building to a climax and resolution?

Sample Outline for Submission to a Company or for Your Own Use

An outline can be one or two pages, depending on what's been requested. Determine the significant events in your plot, and for each event describe the action in one line. List the events in sequential order, according to the plot, and number them. Do not use dialogue, scene headings, or action paragraphs.

CAREER DREAMS--SAMPLE OUTLINE

1. At trendy restaurant, Eva, Grant, and Ana celebrate Eva's promotion to partner in the law firm.

2. At home, Grant and Ana plan a surprise 40th birthday party for Eva when Fran arrives and suggests Eva runs for Congress.

3. Day before party, Ana's concerned by Grant's persistent headaches, but he reassures her he's okay and not to tell Eva who's busy at work and planning congressional run.

4. Morning of Eva's birthday, Ana tries to wake her parents but Grant won't wake up.

5. Grant is rushed to the hospital, but he's already dead.

6. Ana blames Eva for Grant's death and threatens to sabotage her run for Congress.

BEAT SHEET

Like an outline, a beat sheet is a writing tool that illustrates the sequence of major plot events by following your protagonist's journey from beginning to end. Some companies will request you write a beat sheet in order for them to determine if and how your story, characters' arcs, and structure are working.

It's not necessary to write a beat sheet unless a company has requested one. However, writing a beat sheet as an exercise will help you to find the strengths and weaknesses of your story, character's arcs, and structure. It also enables you to see the main turning points in your story.

A beat sheet breaks down your story's structure into literal beats—meaning the major events that occur in your story. A beat sheet should be no longer than one page per act and single-spaced. Each significant event is bulleted and consists of one or two lines of the action. List events in sequential order of the plot's progression. Do not use dialogue, scene headings, or action paragraphs.

CAREER DREAMS--SAMPLE BEAT SHEET

- At a trendy Manhattan restaurant, Eva and her husband, Grant, and their daughter Ana, 13, celebrate Eva's promotion to partner in the law firm. Grant lovingly teases her about her upcoming 40th birthday as Ana giggles.

- That night at their Brooklyn apartment, Grant and Ana plan Eva's surprise 40th birthday party while Eva works in her study. State Senator Fran drops by suggesting Eva run for Congress.

- Day before party, Eva is at work while Ana and Grant make last-minute party preparations. Ana's concerned by Grant's persistent headaches, but he reassures her he's okay and not to tell Eva since she's busy working on a case and her bid for Congress.

- Morning of Eva's birthday, Ana goes to wake her parents but Grant won't wake up; he's not breathing. Ana calls 911 as Eva tries to resuscitate him.

- Grant is rushed to the hospital by ambulance with Eva and Ana at his side, but he's already dead.

- Grief-stricken, Ana blames Eva for Grant's death and threatens to sabotage her run for Congress.

GENRE

"Genre" is the terminology for categorizing a script and/or film. The genre's conventions must be consistent throughout your script; otherwise you will lose the reader. Figure out which category your script fits into on the following Genre List. Pick one—and stick to it!

★ GENRE LIST ★

(Sample list given to story analysts at production companies and studios)

Action
Action Adventure
Action Drama
Adventure
Animated Feature
Biography
Black Comedy
Buddy Movie
Comedy
Coming of Age
Concert
Crime Drama
Disaster
Docudrama
Documentary
Drama
Exploitation
Family
Fantasy
Film Noir
Fish out of Water
Horror
Love Story
Martial Arts
Musical
Musical Comedy
Mystery
One-Person Show
Opera
Romantic Comedy
Satire
Science Fiction
Sexploitation
Slasher
Spoof
Supernatural
Thriller
War
Western

CHARACTERS: GETTING TO KNOW YOU

It is your job to know what makes your characters tick. Writing good dialogue is not enough. Writing new scenes is not enough. You must get inside the minds of your characters. You must know your characters' backgrounds inside and out. Knowing what happened to your characters prior to their appearance in the screenplay will help you to define and create memorable characters. When you really know who your characters are, they will help you solidify your story.

Remember, each character must:

- serve a purpose in your script and push the story forward in some aspect;
- be well defined and fleshed out;
- have a distinct way of speaking so different characters' dialogue is not interchangeable.

QUESTIONS TO ASK YOURSELF ABOUT YOUR CHARACTERS

- Are all of my characters unique? In *Being There* (directed by Hal Ashby, screenplay by Jerzy Kosinski and Robert C. Jones), Chance/Chauncey Gardener is a simple-minded, illiterate gardener whose basic knowledge is acquired from watching and then imitating what he sees on television. Washington's political upper crust applaud his "wisdom" about the garden, misinterpreting his words as poignant metaphors.
- What is my main character's goal in the story? In Alexander Payne's *Election* (written by Payne and Jim Taylor), overachiever Tracy Flick will stop at nothing—she even tears down all of her opponents' posters—to win the student presidential race.

- Are my characters' journeys clear and compelling? In *American Beauty* (directed by Sam Mendes, screenplay by Alan Ball), Lester's midlife crisis—his dysfunctional relationships at home, work, and so on—illustrates his clear and compelling journey.
- What obstacles must my characters face and overcome? In Nora Ephron's *Sleepless in Seattle* (written by Ephron, David S. Ward, and James Arch), Sam's obstacle is overcoming his grief over losing his wife. After a heart-to-heart with her mother, Annie realizes she doesn't feel the magic with her fiancé, Walter, and begins to believe in destiny. Annie's obstacle is facing the suspicion that her fiancé may not be right for her.
- What are my characters' conscious and unconscious desires? In *Big Fish* (directed by Tim Burton, screenplay by John August), Will's conscious and unconscious desires are to distinguish fact from fiction in his father's stories so he can better understand who they both really are.
- What are my characters' hopes and dreams? In *Million Dollar Baby* (directed by Clint Eastwood, screenplay by Paul Haggis), Maggie dreams of becoming a boxer, determined to make something of herself.
- What do my characters learn in the beginning, middle, and end of the script? In Paul and Chris Weitz's film *About a Boy* (screenplay by Peter Hedges, Paul and Chris Weitz), Will, an adult, suffers from Peter Pan syndrome and refers to himself as the island Ibiza. Marcus, the boy, is isolated; he's ostracized at school; and he parents his mother, Fiona, who is isolated in her depression. Will, Marcus, and Fiona transform from isolated loners to relying on each other in a healthy manner—behaving more age appropriately.

- How do my characters change by the end of the script? In director/writer Anthony Minghella's *Cold Mountain*, Ada evolves from helpless southern belle to gritty survivor.
- What are my characters' secrets? In *Catch Me If You Can* (directed by Steven Spielberg, screenplay by Jeff Nathanson), the two main characters have secrets: Frank is a con artist, and Hanratty's family isn't what it appears to be.
- Do my characters have distinctive physical and emotional traits, age, appearances, personalities, intelligence, vulnerabilities, emotions, and idiosyncrasies? In Ridley Scott's *Matchstick Men* (written by Ted and Nicholas Griffin), Roy suffers from tics except when scamming a victim; he's a phobic, a shrewd and manipulative crook, and a "father" who learns to love.
- Will an audience be able to identify with my main character(s)? For example: In Roberto Benigni's *Life Is Beautiful* (cowritten with Vincenzo Cerami), Guido's unstoppable mission to save his son enables the audience to identify with him.
- Have I given the audience a reason to sympathize with my characters? For example: A vulnerable child is harassed by a bully. In *An Angel at My Table* (directed by Jane Campion, screenplay by Laura Jones), we empathize with Janet Frame's survival story by seeing her journey through poverty, family deaths, and misdiagnosis of mental illness to eventually become a confident woman and successful writer.
- Do my characters have specific attitudes toward each other? For example: In director/writer Joel Schumacher's film *Flawless*, two neighbors—Walt, a retired security guard, and Rusty, a street-tough drag queen—are brought together after a series of surprising events. Under their constant sparring and mutual disdain lies a unique respect for each other.

- Do I have a strong antagonist? There's nothing more satisfying to an audience than a fully fleshed-out heavy who is vulnerable, smart, and/or has a sense of humor. In *Silence of the Lambs* (directed by Jonathan Demme, written by Ted Tally), Hannibal Lecter is an involving nemesis because he's emotionally complex and mysterious.
- Does my main character make a decision that leads to a specific action? (For example: Should I pull the trigger? Should I say yes or no?) Seeing characters make decisions under pressure will reveal their true inner motivations. In *John Q* (directed by Nick Cassavetes, written by James Kearns), John makes the decision to hold the ER hostage in order to save his son.
- Are my characters active in my script? Characters can right a wrong, manipulate, scheme, and outsmart others. In director/writer Larry Kasdan's *Body Heat,* Matty, the femme fatale who wants her husband dead, succeeds in manipulating, scheming, and outsmarting her lover, Ned, to achieve her goals.
- What do my characters have to gain or lose? In director/writer Mel Brooks's *The Producers,* if the Broadway show is a flop, Bialystock and Bloom succeed in their scheme; if the show is a success, their scheme fails.
- Do my characters learn something about themselves that they didn't know before? In *Adaptation* (directed by Spike Jonze, written by Charlie Kaufman and "Donald Kaufman"), charming, successful, and superficial Donald becomes a reminder to his twin brother, Charlie, an independent spirit, of what he never wants to become—a Hollywood hack. Charlie later embraces the differences between his twin and himself.

Minor Characters

Minor characters *must* be as unique and as interesting as your major characters. They can be used to reveal information about major characters, which will help you avoid writing exposition. They can also help to push your protagonist's story forward.

For example: In *Hitch* (directed by Andy Tennant, written by Kevin Bisch), the main plot follows the story's central couple, Hitch and Sara. The subplot follows the minor character, Albert, Hitch's client, who is determined to win the affections of the woman of his dreams, celebrity Allegra Cole. Albert is an overweight accountant with two left feet who lacks self-confidence. A minor character, Albert has clear goals and a solid character arc. His character is used to reveal information about Hitch's vulnerabilities when it comes to his own relationships with women, and specifically Sara, thus pushing the protagonist's story forward.

CHARACTER SQUABBLES

Over the years I've had many clients and students argue with me about the need to flesh out their minor characters. They think they don't need to waste their time developing minor characters. Not true! If you don't care about your minor characters, your audience won't. And if they don't care about your minor characters, chances are they won't really care too much for your script. Don't be lazy or sell your script short!

CHARACTER BIO EXERCISE

Whether beginning, rewriting, or polishing a script, our natural instinct is to write only new scenes. New scenes are great, but *characters need your full attention*. The best way to get to know your characters well is to write character bios in their own voices.

1. Write character bios for both your major and minor characters. A bio can be in the form of a letter, an interview, a diary, or whatever format enables you to let loose and write! It can be a few paragraphs or as many pages as you need. Try writing these bios in a stream-of-consciousness format. Write whatever comes into your head about your characters without editing yourself.
2. Have your main characters tell *you* the plot of your script through their eyes. This technique will give you more insight and ideas into your characters and plot, and it will show you what's working and what isn't in your screenplay.
3. Your characters can confide in you. They can tell you their secret thoughts about the other characters, their hopes and dreams, their likes and dislikes, what angers and pleases them, their first loves, their favorite books, their least favorite songs and food, and so on.
4. After you complete the bios, reread your script. Having a clearer understanding and deeper knowledge of your characters will further enhance your screenplay.

PRACTICE WHAT YOU PREACH

I know that I tend to sound like a broken record when I'm telling clients and students about the importance of character bios. I always get a great deal of satisfaction when they tell me later that the bios really helped them in fleshing out their characters and story. I'm delighted. I'm thrilled. And then I feel guilty.

If they could only see me at my computer tackling a rewrite. It's not a pretty sight: all that kicking and screaming and procrastinating because I don't want to spend the time writing another set of character bios.

Once I get over my ridiculous behavior, I sit down and write my bios. My characters become more engaging and unique, and story problems suddenly seem to solve themselves. And then I'm delighted. I'm thrilled. And the guilt vanishes.

EXAMINING YOUR STORY

Every agent and movie executive is looking for a great story. They want to see the innovative ways in which you convey compelling themes, unusual settings, riveting dialogue, and unique and satisfying characters.

How Do I Know If I'm There Yet?

Rewrite your script in short-story form. This will help you determine if you do indeed have a clear narrative structure that divides into three acts (a beginning, a middle, and an end), commanding characters, powerful themes, exceptional settings, and followed the genre's conventions.

QUESTIONS TO ASK YOURSELF ABOUT YOUR STORY

- Have I put a unique twist on my script? For example: My story is inspired by Shakespeare's *Romeo and Juliet*. Have I expressed a distinct perspective on young love and family feuds? In director/writer Neil Jordan's *The Crying Game*, the unique twist lies in Fergus's and Dil's respective secrets: Fergus is responsible for Dil's late boyfriend's death; and Dil is not a woman, she is a man.
- Is my story compelling? Is this a real page-turner? In Joel Schumacher's *Phone Booth* (written by Larry Cohen), the cat-and-mouse game makes this a compelling story. The Caller, a sadistic voyeur, aims his rifle at the slick urban publicist, Stu, and taunts him to confess his sins. It's a page-turner because it poses the questions: Will Stu survive? Will Stu be responsible for the deaths of more people by not following the Caller's instructions?
- Are the stakes clear? What will the characters win or lose? In director/writer Tom Tykwer's *Run Lola Run*, Lola has twenty minutes to come up with the money to save her boyfriend's life from a trigger-happy thug.
- Is the dramatic clock ticking? Regardless of genre, the audience must feel a sense of urgency or expectation in each scene. For example: An anxious groom waits along with the restless guests for the bride's arrival. Where is she? Will the bride get to the church on time? In *Finding Nemo* (directed by Andrew Stanton codirected by Lee Unkrich; written by Andrew Stanton, Bob Peterson, and David Reynolds), Nemo has five days and counting to escape the dentist's fish tank before becoming Darla's pet.

- Do I have a clear subtext? Is my dialogue doing double duty so the audience can read between the lines? Using subtext serves as a way to convey characters' intentions without hitting the audience over the head. In dialogue, for example, a character says one thing, but there's an underlying meaning in what she's saying. In director/writer Joseph L. Mankiewicz's *All About Eve*, Dewitt says to Margo, "Dear Margo. You were an unforgettable Peter Pan. You must play it again soon." The subtext addresses Margo's blatant obsession and fear of aging. (Ageism is also one theme of this film.) Or, in action, what is actually occurring may be perceived in what seems to be occurring. For example, in Act 1 of Clint Eastwood's *Unforgiven* (written by David Webb Peoples), a young bounty hunter known as The Kid offers reformed killer and impoverished hog farmer Bill Munny the opportunity to team up with him. The subtext is illustrated in a sequence of scenes when we see Munny's humiliation and conflicting conscience as he struggles over his decision to join The Kid. Munny's two young children witness their widower father continuously fall face down in the mud, repeatedly and unsuccessfully shoot a tin can, and attempt to get on his horse.
- Does my story have the clear three-act structure common to traditional narrative films? (Act 1: sets up and establishes the story and characters; Act 2: conflicts and obstacles build; Act 3: climax and resolution.)
- If my script has a nonlinear structure, does it serve or detract from my story? In *The Hours* (directed by Stephen Daldry, screenplay by David Hare), this nonlinear structure adds a complex and poignant depth, as seen in the intercutting of the three major storylines: Virginia's, Clarissa's, and Laura's. Each storyline has a well-defined story arc whereby each separate narrative has a distinct beginning, middle, and

end. Virginia's personal life and her book, *Mrs. Dalloway*—and literally its words—profoundly influence both Clarissa's and Laura's respective journeys. As the story reaches its climax, Clarissa's and Laura's narratives converge, and Richard is revealed as Laura's son.

- Am I overexplaining the story by spelling out everything to the point that I'm hitting the audience over the head?
- Have I mistakenly telegraphed in my action paragraph what is about to happen in the forthcoming dialogue or action? For example: "Tara is now ready to talk to Jason because she has a made a decision. Tara: 'I'm ready to talk to you, Jason. I've made a decision.' "
- Are there unexpected occurrences and conflicts that the protagonist must overcome? In Tom Shadyac's *Liar Liar* (screenplay by Paul Guay and Stephen Mazur), the protagonist, Fletcher Reid, a fast-talking lawyer and chronic liar, magically fulfills his son's birthday wish when he must tell the truth for twenty-four hours.
- Does my story continue to build to a climax? In Adrian Lyne's *Unfaithful* (screenplay by Alvin Sargent and William Broyles, Jr.), the story continues to build to a climax. After Edward learns of his wife Connie's affair, he murders her lover, pushing the story to its climax when Connie realizes Edward's guilt.
- Are the ideas that are in my head really on the page? This is a common problem many writers face. Most readers aren't psychic! They don't know your ideas, your intentions, and so on, unless it's clarified on the page.
- Am I conveying and illustrating my story through visuals? *Show,* don't *tell.* Let the audience see clues rather than hearing about them. In *As Good As It Gets* (directed by James L. Brooks, screenplay by Brooks and Mark Andrus),

Melvin Udall suffers from obsessive-compulsive disorder, which is shown rather than discussed. We see his elaborate routine for washing hands, stepping over sidewalk cracks, and bringing his own silverware to restaurants.

- Do I pay off actions that I have set up? You must deliver on this or you will not fulfill the audience's expectations. For example: In the opening of your script a character discovers an ancient artifact. (Your setup.) There must be a ramification to this discovery later on in your script. For example: The artifact contains a secret map, which uncovers a major story clue. (Your payoff.)

There can also be more subtle payoffs to your setups. For example: In *House of Sand and Fog* (directed by Vadim Perelman, screenplay by Perelman and Shawn Otto), the central conflict is ownership of Kathy's house. In the opening of the film, Lester, the cop with whom she later has a relationship, asks Kathy if this is her house, and she says yes. (The setup.) At the end of the film, another police officer asks her if this is her house, and Kathy says no. (The payoff.)

- Hone in on how each scene begins and ends. Get into your scene as late as possible and get out of it as early as possible. This will help the pacing of your script.

DIALOGUE

Sparkling, intelligent, and quick-witted dialogue not only helps enhance the characters but brings life to your story. Characters' dialogue must be distinct and have a unique style, tone, and language. Remember, in real life people rarely speak using stilted, wooden dialogue and formal, complete sentences with perfect grammar. They use contractions, colloquialisms, slang, and verbal shorthand.

Be sure that your characters' voices are not interchangeable. A way to check if your characters have individual voices is to block out your characters' headings. Can you tell who's speaking when you read just the dialogue?

THEMES

The theme is what your story is about. Whether you're writing a thriller or a comedy, stick to your theme! This is your guidepost when creating your script. Almost every scene should reflect your story's theme(s). Characters must evolve and change as the story progresses since this is part of their journey, but your theme(s) must remain constant.

A script may have more than one theme, but be sure that you are not inundating your script with countless themes that don't inform your story and/or characters, or they will confuse the intention of your story. Themes should highlight the action.

There seems to be a tendency to confuse the definitions of theme with plot and loglines, so here are some brief definitions. The plot is the events that make up your story and drive it to its conclusion. The logline is one sentence summarizing the plot.

EXAMPLES OF THEMES

- In *Finding Nemo* (directed by Andrew Stanton and Lee Unkrich; written by Andrew Stanton, Bob Peterson, and David Reynolds), one major theme is dealing with and overcoming fear.
- In *The Fisher King* (directed by Terry Gilliam, screenplay by Richard LaGravenese), one major theme is redemption. Jack and Parry are both in need of redemption. Jack

needs to atone for causing the death of Parry's wife. Parry blames himself for his wife's death, which he had no control over.

- In director/writer Christopher Nolan's *Memento*, the major theme is memory. Leonard's memory loss is the engine that drives the narrative forward, as seen in his attempts to find his wife's killer while others continue to manipulate him. (The title, *Memento,* in Latin means "remember; a reminder of the past.")

FLASHBACKS

Remember that flashbacks are often a red flag for story analysts since this device is often an ineffective shortcut to good storytelling. This device is often overused to repair story and/or character holes and problems, resulting in contrived and inorganic scenes. Occasionally, flashbacks do work successfully, as in Bryan Singer's *The Usual Suspects,* Christopher Nolan's *Memento,* and Quentin Tarentino's film *Jackie Brown,* where they were an integral part of the story structure and storytelling process.

- Relying on flashbacks to tell your story will often slow down the pacing of your script.
- Try to convey relevant information about the past as best you can in the present.

VOICE-OVERS

Use voice-overs only to convey information and insight about the story and/or character(s) that you absolutely cannot convey in dialogue or in action. Examples of films with powerfully effective voice-overs are *Badlands, The Usual Suspects, The Opposite of Sex,* and *American Beauty*. These voice-overs set the tone of the film and get inside the characters' heads in a way that could not have been as effective otherwise.

THE VOICE-OVER GHOSTWRITER

In the mideighties I was hired as a story analyst for a then small company called Miramax Films. Harvey Weinstein was a demanding yet always respectful boss and mentor who generously allowed me the hands-on experience that I needed to learn the industry ropes.

After working at Miramax for several months, I was asked to ghostwrite voice-over narrations for several completed films that they had purchased from outside companies for distribution. Why did they need a ghostwriter? These acquired films had a name cast and marketing potential, but the stories had big holes in them. Sometimes story questions were raised but never answered, leaving the audience confused. Other times, character motivations were not grounded or realistic to the story.

Rather than going to great expense to reshoot scenes, often the best solution was to simply add a voice-over. It was my job to answer all those story questions, filling in the blanks. In doing so, I would choose a character, get inside his or her head (by writing numerous character bios), and then write a narration addressing these issues.

It was important that the voice-over have a distinctive

style yet remain true to the character already presented on-screen. After the written narration was completed, the actor was called in to a postproduction house to record the voice-over, which would then be added to the film.

A *Variety* review praised one of these films that I had ghostwritten, lauding the unique spin the voice-over narration had given to the story.

GRABBING THE READER'S ATTENTION IN YOUR FIRST TEN PAGES

Your script must be engaging from page one, paragraph one. Story analysts, competition judges, and executives are tireless readers, but don't put them to sleep because they're bored or frustrated with your script. There's nothing more satisfying than discovering a great talent, but there's nothing more aggravating than wasting time on a script that doesn't deliver.

A JUDGE'S SECRET

In my experience as a script competition judge, often we are asked to read only the first ten pages of a script. Given this fact, be sure that your first ten pages (as well as the remainder of your script) are gripping.

QUESTIONS TO ASK YOURSELF ABOUT YOUR FIRST TEN PAGES

- Have I clearly established the genre? If the reader is questioning whether your script is a comedy or a drama, then you haven't done your job.

- Have I set the stage uniquely? In the first eight minutes of *Atlantic City* (directed by Louis Malle, screenplay by John Guare), a vast amount of information is quickly and succinctly conveyed through visual storytelling: (1) the main characters are introduced in their distinctive work and home environments; and (2) the unique setting is established as we see the old Atlantic City being demolished to make way for the new Atlantic City.
- Every story begins with the question "What if?" Have I posed this question succinctly? In Stephen Spielberg's *E.T. the Extra-Terrestrial* (screenplay by Melissa Mathison) the story opens with the question: What if an extraterrestrial landed in a young boy's backyard and the young boy decides to hide him?
- Does my script open with a gripping event? For example: A wedding, a funeral, a murder, someone leaving, or someone arriving. In Ridley Scott's *Thelma and Louise* (screenplay by Callie Khouri), the opening scenes center on Thelma and Louise about to embark on their fateful two-day trip.
- Is it clear who my protagonist is and what his or her need or desire is? In Joan Chen's *Xiu Xiu: The Sent-Down Girl* (written by Chen and Geling Yan) Xiu Xiu, is clearly established as the protagonist who is in desperate need of finding a way to return home to her family.
- Does my script answer the question, "Why is today different than any other day for my main characters?" In *My Best Friend's Wedding* (directed by P.J. Hogan, screenplay by Ronald Bass), today is different from any other day when Julianne gets a phone call from her best friend, Michael, who tells her that he's getting married.
- Is my story in progress? Will the reader ask, "What's going to happen next?" In *Salaam Bombay!* (directed by Mira

Nair, written by Nair and Sooni Taraporevala), Krishna's constant struggle to survive against insurmountable obstacles, as he attempts to earn money to return home to his family, poses the question, "What's going to happen next to Krishna, and will he achieve his goal?"

- Are my environments clearly established? Do not set your story in "Any City" unless this is a specific story choice you are making. Characters must relate to their environment, and in turn this must influence the story. For example, setting your script in Atlanta or in a small town in New Mexico will help to define what your story is about and how your characters will relate to this specific environment. If your main character is originally from Manhattan and is now living in a small rural town in Wisconsin, the character's relationship to the environment should be specific. (For example: How is your gritty New Yorker going to cope with needing to milk a cow in order to survive?) The audience must enter this world with a complete understanding of it.

In director/writer Sofia Coppola's *Lost in Translation,* the specific setting of Tokyo, the Japanese culture and customs, and Bob and Charlotte's relationship to Tokyo, clearly establish the setting and are integral to the plot. The story centers on this couple who otherwise would have little in common if they weren't Americans drawn together by their simultaneous coping with this foreign culture.

FORMATTING

Film executives expect you to abide by the strict industry formatting rules and regulations. Poor formatting is a sign of an amateur! Don't risk having your script rejected due to incorrect or sloppy formatting. Be sure that your screenplay is specific enough so the reader is clear about your vision. However, this does not mean that you should dictate camera angles. This is the director's job and is considered unacceptable in industry-standard screenplay formatting.

If you're looking to invest in screenwriting software, read screenwriting publications as well as the WGA Web site at www.wga.org. If you can't afford to purchase software and need a more detailed explanation, here are two books I recommend: Hillis R. Cole with Judith H. Haag's *The Complete Guide to Standard Script Formats: Part I: Screenplays* and/or *Elements of Style for Screenwriters,* by Paul Argentini. These books can be found in bookstores or online.

Unless otherwise requested, when you submit your script, do not include a separate page listing your characters and their descriptions, your résumé, budget, or casting ideas.

FREQUENTLY ASKED QUESTIONS

My screenplay opens with my protagonist, Rachel, as a young girl, then jumps ahead to the future when Rachel is an adult, and then moves back again to when she's young. How do I identify her in the character headings and action paragraphs?

Rachel as a young girl should be consistently identified as "YOUNG RACHEL" in your character headings and "Young Rachel" in your action paragraphs. Rachel as an adult should be consistently identified as "ADULT RACHEL" in your character headings and "Adult Rachel" in your action paragraphs. Remember, when Young Rachel and Adult Rachel are first seen, their names should be in CAPS.

My character, Justin, is impersonating someone named Aaron, but I don't know the proper way to indicate this in my screenplay.

You have two choices: "JUSTIN/AARON" or "JUSTIN AS AARON" for character headings, or "Justin/Aaron" or "Justin as Aaron" in your action paragraphs. Whichever one you choose, you must consistently use the same choice throughout your script.

Your Screenplay

BASIC FORMATTING CHECKLIST

- Don't use camera angles.
- Don't use scene numbers. Scene numbers are used for shooting scripts only.
- Number all your script pages on the top right.
- The title page is not numbered.
- Avoid breaking up dialogue between pages.
- Single space dialogue and action paragraphs.
- Writing "MORE" or "CONTINUED" on the bottom of each page is not necessary.
- Speaking characters should have a brief description that includes: approximate age, how they look, and personality traits. (For example: Ana, 13, all hormones and rage, wears Goth garb and a smirk.)
- POV: Use sparingly to indicate a character's point of view or from what angle we see the action occur.

TITLE PAGE CHECKLIST

- Do not number this page.
- This page, as well as the rest of your script, must be in twelve-point Courier font.

- The script's title is in CAPS and is centered one-third below the top of the page.
- Use: "Screenplay by" or "by." This is centered three single line spaces below the script's title. (No CAPS.)
- The screenwriter's name is centered three single line spaces below "Screenplay by" or "by." (No CAPS.)
- The screenwriter's name, address, phone number, fax, and e-mail should appear in the lower right-hand corner, single-spaced. If you have an agent, then the agent's name and contact information is used there instead. (Your agent must give you the okay to submit scripts on your own and will tell you how to format the cover page with the agency's information.)
- Include the WGA registration and copyright date, centered on the bottom of the page. (Do not include a copy of the WGA registration receipt with your script. This is your receipt only.)
- Do not include draft dates and/or draft numbers on your spec script cover, unless you've been asked to do so.
- You might be a talented visual artist, but don't put a graphic on the cover page, since this screams amateur.

WHEN TO CAPITALIZE

- Use CAPS for: Scene headings (slug lines) and character headings. Sound effects and important clues can also be capped, but this is optional.
- CAP a character's name *only* when the character is first seen (not referred to in dialogue or seen in a photograph) in the screenplay.
- CAP the first letter only if the character continues in the scene or appears in other scenes to follow. For example: "ANA" (in CAPS when she is first seen in your script) and

"Ana" (not in CAPS when she is seen thereafter). When characters don't have a name, use a description. For example: "WAITER" (in CAPS when he is first seen) and "Waiter" (not in CAPS when he is seen thereafter).

ACTION PARAGRAPHS

- Do not capitalize, underline, or italicize all the words.
- Do not indent.
- Use present tense only.
- Avoid verbs ending in "-ing." Doing so will help your action paragraphs to be more succinct; fewer words will be needed. For example: "Jane is throwing the ball to John" can be revised to: "Jane throws the ball to John." In addition, using this method assists writers who have trouble keeping the action lines in the present tense.
- Do not include characters' feelings or thoughts.
- Keep action paragraphs to four lines or less.
- Break up the action of different characters into their own action lines. Remember, readers often quickly scan the page so you want to make it as easy a read as possible.
- Each new scene must have a scene heading (for example: "EXT. FARM - DAY"). Underneath the scene heading in your action paragraph, describe the setting and indicate the characters' actions.
- When a scene changes from one location to another use a new scene heading.

PRINTING OUT, BINDING, AND MAILING YOUR SCRIPT TIPS

Printing Out Your Script

Print out your script using a good letter-quality printer! If you don't have a good printer, then go to a store that can professionally print out your script. It's worth the investment. Readers hate smudges, faint print, inadvertent printer lines through the text, and so on. Use only white paper and black ink.

Before you make copies, read through each page of your script very carefully to make sure that the ink hasn't clogged. Each and every letter on your clean white page should be clear and easy to read.

The Right Paper to Use

Use three-hole punch, 8½" × 11", standard white twenty pound bond paper.

How to Bind Your Script

Use roundheaded brass fasteners known as brads, which are the industry standard: 1¼ inches for scripts up to hundred pages; 1½ or 2 inches for scripts more than hundred pages.

Most screenwriting publications advertise companies that sell brads. (*See the appendix on page 257.*) Use the right size! I've received countless scripts with the wrong-size brads, and the script tears or falls apart.

Don't use notebooks, or spiral bindings. Use only the fasteners.

Don't tape the ends of the brads to the script. Often readers and executives unfasten the script because they prefer reading it unbound and/or they want to make copies of the script for associates in their company.

There's an ongoing debate whether to use two or three brads to bind a script. (If you choose to use two brads, then fasten one on the top and one on the bottom of your script.) Personally, I find three brads to be more secure, since two brads often make the script buckle and the pages come unbound. Either choice is industry acceptable.

The Script Cover: What to Use and Do You Really Need It?

Whether you choose to use a script cover is up to you. Either way, it won't jeopardize your script's chances with a prospective reader. It's used to protect your script from any damage.

If you decide to use a script cover, select the same colored card stock (65 pound to 110 pound) for the front and back of your script. Bind the front and back script cover using brads—the same as you would if you didn't use a cover. The front and back covers should not have any writing on them.

The Mailing Envelope

Submitting a script in a padded envelope or a Priority Mail envelope is more expensive, but it's safer. Standard envelopes tend to tear and are more flimsy. Be sure that your script fits comfortably into the envelope to avoid tears.

CHAPTER FIVE

THE QUEST FOR A WINNING QUERY LETTER

FINDING AND UNLOCKING THE SECRET DOOR

A good query letter is your key to unlocking an executive's door. Writing queries can be a painstaking process. Take your time and be as thoughtful about your query as you were when writing your screenplay.

Query letters must have punch to entice the agent, producer, production company, and/or studio to want to read your screenplay. (As noted in chapter 10, you may still continue to query production companies, studios, and/or talent once you have an agent.) Your enthusiasm and passion about your project must shine through in your query.

A query letter serves three main purposes: (1) it opens the door to establishing a relationship with an executive; (2) it requests permission to legally submit your screenplay; and (3) it creates a paper trail, which provides a written record of everywhere it has been submitted in the event there is a dispute over theft of ideas.

Industry professionals view query letters as a reflection of the writer's screenplay and writing skills. So the assumption will be if the query letter is poor, then the script will be, too.

Remember, if you continue to get rejections or no response from your query, there may be a good reason for it. Your query isn't doing the job!

FREQUENTLY ASKED QUESTIONS

How long should the query letter be?

One page only.

What should my query letter include?

It should include an opening paragraph, a one-sentence logline, one paragraph about the project, one paragraph about your background, and one paragraph inviting the agent and/or executive to read your script. You should also include a self-addressed, stamped envelope (SASE) for the recipient's response.

Where do I find agents, production companies, and/or studios to query?

Many screenwriting publications include information about who's currently accepting queries. In addition, look for the WGA Guild Signatory Agents and Agencies List on their Web site: www.wga.org. You can also purchase the Hollywood Agents and Managers Directory. If you are looking for production companies, one of the most reliable resources is the Hollywood Creative Directory. *(See the appendix on page 257 for the aforementioned publications and others listings.)*

How do I start the querying process?

1. Develop a marketing plan. If you are looking for an agent, target the Los Angeles and New York agen-

cies first. If you are looking for a producer, production company, and/or studio for your project, find out what types of projects they are looking for and what they have produced in the past. Make sure your project is a match; otherwise you're wasting your time.

2. Target about twenty companies to start with.
3. Send out the twenty queries and see what type of response you get. If you are not getting any positive feedback, then rewrite your query before targeting the next twenty companies on your list.

Should I call every agent, producer, production company, and/or studio on my list prior to sending my query?

Unfortunately, the answer is yes if you want results. It's important to know the submission policy of the agency, producer, production company, and/or studio so your query shows your film-industry savvy. Certainly this is time-consuming and will run up your phone bill, but it's well worth the investment.

Calls will give you the opportunity to make personal connections to the receptionists and assistants. Keep in mind that today's assistant or receptionist may be tomorrow's agent or executive. A kind letter and/or call may be very welcome to assistants who are often overworked, underpaid, and not appreciated.

If you're looking for representation, you should ask which agent is looking for new writers. If you're calling a producer, production company, or studio, you should ask what types of projects they are seeking. Also, you can verify the correct spelling and title of the person you are querying. This is crucial because there is a revolving door of executives in the film industry.

To whom should I address my query?

It's best to call and find out the appropriate contact person and verify the correct spelling of his or her name and title. Many writers make the mistake of addressing their queries to the president of a studio or even "To Whom It May Concern." This will show that you're not savvy and your query will most likely be thrown out.

How long will it take to get a response to my queries?

The reply time may be several weeks. If a month passes, you may call and ask if they have received your query and/or send another letter stating that this is your second query. If there is no response, assume that they are not interested and move on to the next person or company on your list. Also, you may not hear back if you have forgotten to include an SASE.

Is it acceptable to fax or e-mail my query?

Most companies prefer a mailed query because they may want to use the SASE to respond and/or enclose a release form if they are interested in reading your script. Call the company and ask what they prefer.

Should I enclose a postcard along with my query for a response?

A postcard with a box to check: "Yes, I want to read your script" or "No, I don't want to read your script" is acceptable, but some companies prefer you not do this. Find out their preference. If the company does prefer this method, be sure to enclose an SASE so an agent, a producer, a production company, and/or a studio can send you a release form.

Who reads my query?

Usually an assistant will read the query letter first. If the assistant deems the query to be of interest to the company and does not have the power to make a decision, he or she will pass it on to the executive. If the executive is interested in your project, you will be asked to submit your synopsis, treatment, and or/screenplay.

What if I don't have any film—or writing-related experience?

If you have taken a professional and notable writing or film course, then include this in your query. If you have no experience at all, you may want to state what profession you are in, the college you attended, or what inspired you to write your screenplay by briefly stating how it specifically relates to your story. You might spark interest by including the aforementioned suggestions. For example, the person reading your query may have gone to the same college and this may help to establish a personal connection. Generally, few executives are truly interested in your personal background and may be turned off to read this. However, when I suggested to my clients who didn't have any film- or writing-related experience to include one or two references about their personal backgrounds in their queries, some did receive requests to read their scripts. If you decide to choose any of these options, keep it very brief!

How do I know if the production company I am querying is legitimate?

Trust your gut instinct and do your research. Learn what films the company has produced, what it currently has in development, and if it has a production deal with a studio and/or some type of financing. Reading trade publications and online message boards will also help in your research. *(See the appendix on page 257.)*

Do I need a personal recommendation?

A personal recommendation, also known as an "industry referral," is seen as a confirmation from another industry professional that your script has potential. It also shows that you are savvy and have some connections. But if you don't have any personal connections, don't despair. Writing a winning query will get you in the door.

If I have won a script competition, should I include this in my query?

Yes. If you have won or placed as a finalist in a reputable screenplay contest, definitely include this in your query.

Should I summarize the story of my script by referring to my successful films?

Film executives tend to differ as to whether or not a writer should refer to his or her successful films. Some executives want to see that you've written a unique project that has never been seen before, while others like to see how your project will fit into their marketing scheme. Trust your instincts.

Should I state in my query that I have written other scripts aside from the one that I'm querying them about?

Stating that you've written several scripts is fine, but listing ten or so may be a detriment. The agent or executive may see this as a negative and be concerned that nothing thus far has happened with your other scripts.

If I have already had production companies and/or studios read my script, should I include this in my query to agents?

Some agents feel that this is a positive since you are illustrating initiative, while others feel that you are limiting their playing field with your project if it has already been read. This is your call. Literally. Calling ahead and asking is your best bet.

What if an agent I have queried wants to read my script but charges a reading fee?

Never pay a reading fee. Agents who are WGA signatories cannot charge a fee. You want an agent who is signatory because he or she must abide by the WGA rules, which protect writers' interests.

Should I send a synopsis or résumé with my query?

No. Send only your query letter unless you have spoken to the agency, producer, studio, or production company first and they have requested additional material from you. If you do include additional material without being asked for it, this will be seen as unprofessional, and you will risk having the query tossed out.

Should I print out my query on fancy stationery or design a logo?

Most agents and executives prefer a standard, no-frills business letter. They often feel that writers spend too much time on design and not enough time on content. It's the content that's going to win them over in the end!

How do I know if my query is ready to be sent out?

If possible, have it read by an industry professional or someone whose opinion you respect and get feedback. Ask them if the query was enticing enough for them to want to read your script. Be sure to have it proofread!

QUERY LETTER DO'S

- Be original. Your query must stand out in the crowd. It should show the reader who you are.
- Be brief and to the point. This is a business letter; don't be chatty.
- Express confidence in your work and ability.
- Synopsize your script in approximately five succinct sentences, following your protagonist's journey. Stick to only the important story points.
- The synopsis should be in the present tense. Avoid passive verbs.
- The synopsis should be active and dramatic.
- Be sure that your story concept is clear.
- Include a one-sentence logline.
- Use short paragraphs.
- Be sure to indicate the genre of your script.
- Provide information about who you are and any film- or writing-related background you may have. Be honest!
- Provide your contact information. If you're going to be moving, then mention when your new contact information will be in effect.
- Enclose an SASE.
- Keep a copy of your query for your files, as well as a list of whom you submit your letters to.

- Always call ahead to confirm that the person you are submitting to is still working in that position and to confirm spellings, titles, and guidelines.
- Before mailing your query, double check that your envelope is addressed to the same person as your query.

QUERY LETTER DON'TS

- No typos. No grammatical errors. No incorrect punctuation. No smudges.
- Don't handwrite your letter.
- Don't begin with "To Whom It May Concern." Get the addressee's name and title. Spell it correctly!
- When addressing your query, don't use an agent's executive's first name unless you know him or her very well.
- Don't flatter the addressee too much.
- Don't sell yourself short.
- Don't include too much plot description.
- Don't reveal your script's ending.
- Don't beg.
- Don't ask for permission to send your script.
- Don't include casting or box-office projections.
- Don't be obnoxiously funny or too cute to attract attention.
- Don't state your theme(s). If you do your job well, this will be evident.
- Don't repeat your logline in your synopsis.
- Don't say that your script is great; your logline and synopsis should say it all.
- Don't include your ideas on how your script should be marketed.
- Don't include your script's budget.

- Don't send a form letter. Your query must be specific to each individual.

MILLION-DOLLAR SCRIPT

"My script will make a hundred million dollars at the box office" "I'm confident that Tom Cruise and Madonna will want to play the lead parts." "This is the best script that you'll ever read." You can laugh, but these are actual examples of queries that I received from anxious screenwriters when I was working in studio and production company development offices. Yes, your project may make millions of dollars, and even attract Tom Cruise and Madonna to star, and it may be the best script an executive has ever read—but there are no guarantees. Promoting yourself and your project in this manner is not a savvy way to grab an executive's attention.

LOGLINES

A logline is a written pitch that is one sentence long. "Logline" literally refers to the process by which a script is logged in at an agency, a production company, or a studio's office once a story analyst completes the coverage. (*See chapter 3, "Coverage."*)

Some companies and agents differ as to the necessity of including a logline in a query, but I would suggest doing so.

You must work as hard on your logline as you did on

your script. Impress the executive with your writing craft. You want the executive to request your script now!

A common problem that I've seen with clients' and students' loglines is that they are too vague. Loglines must clearly and succinctly convey what the core of your story is about, using your story arc as your guide. The first step is to ask yourself: "What is my script about?" and then answer the question.

A logline is not a tagline, as seen in a movie trailer or movie advertisement.

LOGLINE DO'S

- Use present tense. It's more exciting and immediate.
- Grab the reader's attention from word one.
- Every word must do double duty. Less is more.
- Accurately describe your story and setting, your protagonist, and his or her major goal and conflict/obstacle.
- Show the reader how your story is different and unique, and what sets it apart.
- Your protagonist must be one with whom an audience can identify.
- Define who your protagonist is. For example, include your protagonist's profession.
- Indicate how your characters are distinct by using a strong adjective to describe them.

LOGLINE DON'TS

- Don't inundate the reader with useless information or get bogged down in story and/or character details.
- Don't use the phrase "It's a story about . . ." It's too wordy.

- Don't use the phrase "We follow the journey of . . ." This doesn't tell us what the story is about, and it's too wordy.
- Don't use metaphors.
- Don't be cagey or cute.
- Don't include characters' names.
- Don't write a run-on sentence.
- Don't use passive verbs, which are verbs ending in "-ing."

LOGLINE EXAMPLES

The following three loglines show you the do's and don'ts for writing a successful logline.

Unsuccessful Logline Example #1

Will Sammy overcome his demons before it's too late?

WHY IT'S UNSUCCESSFUL

- It sounds like a movie trailer.
- It doesn't tell us what the story is about or what the major conflict is.
- The phrase "too late" doesn't tell us what's at stake in your story.
- It includes the character's name, which loglines should not.
- Sammy could be male, female, a child, a teen, or an adult.
- It doesn't tell us who Sammy really is.

Unsuccessful Logline Example #2

It's a story about a teacher who learned life lessons as she discovered the meaning of life.

WHY IT'S UNSUCCESSFUL

- It's written in the past tense.
- "It's a story about" is too wordy and unnecessary.
- We don't know what type of teacher or person she is.
- "Learns life lessons" and "discovering the meaning of life" identifies the themes of the story. (A logline must not include the theme of your script; it should be evident.)
- It doesn't tell us what the story is about or what major obstacle she must overcome.
- It repeats the word "life."

Successful Logline Example

Seeking justice for her husband's untimely death, a resolute Manhattan attorney runs for Congress despite her manipulative teenage daughter's sabotage.

WHY IT'S SUCCESSFUL

- It leaps into the story. It's succinct. Every word counts.
- It tells us what the story is about: The protagonist's husband's untimely death compels her to run for Congress, which presents the major obstacle: her choice to run for office despite her manipulative teenage daughter's sabotage.
- "Seeking justice for her husband's untimely death" defines the protagonist's major plot goal. It informs us that she's a proactive widow with a mission. "Untimely death" prompts the reader to ask, "How did he die?"
- The mother/daughter conflict is illustrated by including two important adjectives that describe each character: "resolute" for the protagonist and "manipulative" for the teenage daughter.

- Including the noun "sabotage" details the mother/daughter conflict and specifies that the daughter's actions against her mother are deliberate.
- We learn the protagonist's profession in one word—"attorney"—which suggests that her background could make her a suitable congressional candidate.
- Using "teenage" and "daughter" defines the daughter much better than "kid," which does not give her approximate age or gender.
- The urban setting of "Manhattan" is established in one word.

QUERY LETTER CONTENT

Remember, assistants and executives are pressed for time, so you must be succinct, make every word count, and demonstrate your solid writing skills so they will eagerly request your work. Accurately represent your project and who you are!

Your query letter should stress how your script will meet the executive's needs, not vice versa.

BEGGING AND PLEADING

Several years ago I had a very talented client who was diligently working on a screenplay. When the script was ready for submission, she showed me a sample of her query letter. It was an honest assessment of her life, but perhaps too honest.

The letter went something like this:

Dear Company:

I am married with a four-year-old daughter and am currently working at a sales job. My husband is in graduate school and we are living with his parents to save money. I am under a great deal of pressure to earn a better salary. I love to write and really want to make a living as a screenwriter. If you have some time and have any interest in my story idea, will you consider reading my script?

QUERY LETTER CHECKLIST

- A query should be in a professional business-letter format.
- No fancy fonts.
- Use standard white 20-pound. bond paper.
- Use a standard white #10 business envelope.
- Fold letter in thirds with the addressee's name, title, and address facing up.
- If an enclosure has been requested, fold the two pages as one.
- The SASE can be folded in thirds.

A QUERY LETTER THAT WORKS

Your query letter must grab the attention of industry professionals who read countless queries daily. Show your solid writing skills and specifically tailor it to each company and/or individual.

The following is a template of a basic query letter. You don't have to strictly adhere to this template; you can be inventive.

```
Date

Executive's name
Executive's title
Address of company

Dear Mr. or Ms. Executive: (use a colon, not
comma)

Begin with a friendly greeting and/or
attention-grabbing line about your script.
Continue with a sentence such as: "I have
just completed the feature screenplay that I
would like to submit to you for your
consideration." Choose an opening that best
suits your script and reflects who you are
as a writer. If appropriate, include
information about why your project may be
the right match for their company.

One-sentence logline.

Synopsize your script in approximately five
sentences. State the genre (here or in your
opening paragraph), who the main characters
are (using their actual names), what their
major obstacle is, and how they plan to
overcome it. Don't give away the ending.
```

Give a brief one-paragraph bio stressing your screenwriting or film background. For example: "I am a recent graduate of" or "My credits include: (name films or scripts and awards)." You may want to add something unique about yourself that makes you attractive to the executive. (See above FAQs in this chapter.)

Closing paragraph. Two to three simple sentences will do. For example: "Thank you very much for your consideration. Enclosed you will find a self-addressed, stamped envelope for your reply. I look forward to hearing from you soon."

Sincerely,

Name
Address
Phone number
Fax number
E-mail address

Query Sample #1

Query Sample #1 is the most "traditional" example. It closely follows the previous template.

Date

Executive's name
Executive's title
Address

Dear Ms. Executive:

I have just completed *Career Dreams*, a feature-length screenplay that I would like to submit to you for your consideration. Given the successful family dramas you've produced, I believe this script shares your company's sensibilities.

Logline: Seeking justice for her husband's untimely death, a resolute Manhattan attorney runs for Congress despite her manipulative teenage daughter's sabotage.

Career Dreams soon become career nightmares when Eva Gomez, 40, a Manhattan attorney, discovers that her husband's death was due to medical malpractice. Determined to change the laws, she makes the decision to run for Congress. But Ana, 13, all hormones and rage, doesn't want her mom to become center stage, and she's hell-bent on sabotaging Eva's chances for political office. Torn between Ana's grief and self-centeredness, and her own desire to protect patients' rights, Eva must find a way to achieve a renewed relationship with Ana as she attempts to achieve her goals.

Career Dreams won the (state year)
Famous Screenwriter award and placed as
a semifinalist at the (state year)
City Scripts competition. *Times One*,
my feature-length comedy, won the
Funniest Screenwriter Award last year.
I am a journalist with an M.F.A.
in Screenwriting from Great University,
and a B.A. from Great College.

Thank you very much for your consideration.
Enclosed please find a self-addressed,
stamped envelope for your reply. I look
forward to hearing from you soon.

Sincerely,

Susan Savvy
Address
Phone number
Fax number
E-mail address

Query Sample #2

Query Sample #2 is less "traditional" than the template on pages 122–23.

It opens with information about the protagonist in boldface type for emphasis. It's specifically geared to a star's production company. Stating "Having just read in the trades that your company is seeking family dramas with a powerful lead" shows that the writer is industry savvy by reading the trades and knows that what this specific company is seeking includes the project's genre. The biography paragraph cites relevant background and knowledge of the script's subject matter: a Manhattan attorney with a degree minor in investigative journalism. Stating the names of the university and writing programs attended gives the writer with no screenwriting or film credits some credibility. It also opens the door for a possible personal connection to the university and/or writing program the writer attended.

Date

Executive's name
Executive's title
Address

Dear Ms. Executive:

Meet Eva Gomez. Recent widow. Successful lawyer. Unsuccessful mother. Desperate for justice.

Having just read in the trades that your company is seeking family dramas with a powerful female lead, I believe the role of Eva Gomez in my feature-length screenplay

Career Dreams is a perfect match for (fill in star's name).

Logline: Seeking justice for her husband's untimely death, a resolute Manhattan attorney runs for Congress despite her manipulative teenage daughter's sabotage.

Career Dreams soon become career nightmares when Eva Gomez, 40, a Manhattan attorney, discovers that her husband's death was due to medical malpractice. Determined to change the laws, she makes the decision to run for Congress. But Ana, 13, all hormones and rage, doesn't want her mom to become center stage, and she's hell-bent on sabotaging Eva's chances for political office. Torn between Ana's grief and self-centeredness, and her own desire to protect patients' rights, Eva must find a way to achieve a renewed relationship with Ana as she attempts to achieve her goals.

I am a malpractice attorney in Manhattan and received my law degree at Great University, where I also minored in investigative journalism. I have taken numerous screenwriting courses at Name University.

Thank you very much for your consideration. Enclosed please find a self-addressed,

stamped envelope for your reply. I look
forward to hearing from you soon.

Sincerely,

Susan Savvy
Address
Phone number
Fax number
E-mail address

Query Sample #3

Query Sample #3 is less traditional than the template on pages 122–23. It opens with questions from the antagonist's point of view, and the questions are in boldface type for emphasis. This query is specifically geared to a screenwriting agent. Including "and understand that you are currently seeking new writers" shows that the writer has done her research about this agency. The biography section comes before the logline and synopsis to emphasize the writer's credits.

Date

Executive's name
Executive's title
Address

Dear Ms. Executive:

What do you hate more? Injustice? Death? Your mother? All of the above?

For Ana Whitman all of the above doesn't even begin to cover it. She's thirteen. And she'll stop at nothing to prevent her mother from achieving her goal.

Bring mother and daughter together and witness this family drama in my feature-length screenplay, *Career Dreams*, which I would like to submit for your consideration. I am seeking representation and understand that you are currently seeking new writers.

Career Dreams won the (state year) Famous Screenwriter award and placed as a finalist at the (state year) City Scripts competition. *Times One*, my feature-length comedy, won the Funniest Screenwriter award last year. I received my Bachelor of Arts degree from Name University.

Logline: Seeking justice for her husband's untimely death, a resolute Manhattan attorney runs for Congress despite her manipulative teenage daughter's sabotage.

Career Dreams soon become career nightmares when Eva Gomez, 40, a Manhattan attorney, discovers that her husband's death was due to medical malpractice. Determined to change the laws, she makes the decision to run for Congress. But Ana, 13, all hormones and rage, doesn't want her mom to become center stage, and she's hell-bent on sabotaging Eva's chances for political office. Torn between Ana's grief and self-centeredness, and her own desire to protect patients' rights, Eva must find a way to achieve a renewed relationship with Ana as she attempts to achieve her goals.

Thank you very much for your consideration. Enclosed please find a self-addressed, stamped envelope for your reply. I look forward to hearing from you soon.

Sincerely,

Susan Savvy
Address
Phone number
Fax number
E-mail address

CHAPTER SIX

SHARPENING YOUR SYNOPSIS

WHY YOU NEED TO WRITE A SYNOPSIS

Your synopsis is the tool that will prompt an agent, a studio, a producer, and/or a production company to request your script. Why? Executives are inundated with scripts, and a synopsis is a quick way for them to determine if your project may be of interest. Generally, if you get a positive response from your query, the next step may be a request for your synopsis and/or your screenplay. Given this, your synopsis must be solid and reflect your talents as a writer.

WISHING ON A STAR

A couple of years ago, a development executive from a prominent production company contacted me to see if I had any projects appropriate for them. (It's always a bonus to have an executive call you seeking material rather than vice versa!)

The executive listed the following parameters they were seeking:

- A script that was ready to go. (Meaning that it was a completed script and not in progress.)
- Low or medium budget. (Their preference was under $10 million.)
- A strong role for the star. (This production company was set up to produce projects for this well-known male actor, and they were looking for a starring vehicle for him.)
- Character-driven. (No action, sci-fi, or period pieces.)
- Location. (New York City area was preferable.)
- Registered with the WGA.

The executive stated that if I had any scripts that applied, she wanted to read the synopses. I had three projects I thought might be appropriate, and per her request I faxed her the three synopses. Within minutes she responded, requesting to read all three scripts. Hence, the moral of the story: Write a sensational synopsis! The good news: they liked all three scripts. They chose one script that they felt was a perfect match for the star and they were about to option it when the bad news came—the star had suddenly become critically ill and could no longer act in films.)

Writing a synopsis can also be useful when you are polishing your script. It helps you to determine if your story line is clear and if your main character's journey is compelling.

The process of writing a synopsis can often be frustrating. Be patient! It's important to take your time and use that same creative energy as you did when writing your screenplay.

ELATION, INTERRUPTED

You've finished your script and you're elated! You're ready for the world to see your script and to start making contacts with companies and agents. But the last thing you want to do now is to write a synopsis. I know. I've been there. And I know what you're thinking: "How can I convey what my script is about in only one page?"

My clients and students always try to convince me that their amazing scripts will grab an executive's attention, and that spending so much time writing a strong synopsis isn't that necessary. Unfortunately, they're wrong. Yes, writing a synopsis is grueling work, but it must be done—and done well.

Often my clients will submit a synopsis along with their script and ask me to analyze both. I always read their synopsis first. I am usually quite impressed with the story and style in which these synopses have been written. But when I then read their scripts, I'm often dismayed that they do not reflect the information, style, or story accurately. There are missing plot points and character inconsistencies, but, most important, the synopsis fails to convey the tone of the script. (The synopsis may read like a comedy when the script is really a drama.)

Be sure that your synopsis accurately reflects your script. Ask a few people who haven't read your script to read your synopsis and then ask them what your story is about. Their feedback should accurately describe your script. If not, you haven't done your job.

QUESTIONS TO ASK ABOUT YOUR SYNOPSIS

- Is my synopsis an interesting and compelling read?
- Do my protagonist and antagonist have clear journeys and solid arcs?
- Were the genre conventions followed?
- Were the conflicts between my protagonist and antagonist clear?
- Were the stakes in the story clear?
- Were there any places that you were confused, lost, and/or bored?
- Was the setting and time period clearly conveyed?
- Did I clearly set the stage and create the world of my story?

FREQUENTLY ASKED QUESTIONS

How long should the synopsis be?

Most agents, production companies, and studios want one page only. Find out specific policies prior to submission.

Can I include a dialogue sample within the synopsis?

If the dialogue sample is brief and will give the reader an insightful clue to your character(s), then this is acceptable.

Should I describe my character using a movie star's name?

Some executives feel it's best not to describe your character using a movie star's name because it takes away from the originality of your character and/or script. Other executives like to get a clear picture of what you have in mind. For example, "Martin Andrews, a Tom Hanks–type everyman, . . ."

Should I reveal the ending?

Some executives differ on this, but generally the answer is no. Your goal is to entice the reader to request your script.

YOUR SYNOPSIS SHOULD:

- accurately reflect your story and characters;
- illustrate your writing style as well as the style of your script;
- be brief, energetic, and to the point;
- be written in the present tense;
- stay focused on your protagonist's journey and character arc;
- describe the main plot of your script;
- contain information about genre, setting, and time period;
- clearly set the stage and create the world for the reader;
- illustrate what makes your story and characters distinct;
- establish what's at stake for your main characters;
- use clear, concise sentences and active verbs;
- use the main characters' names;
- indicate the passage of time when crucial to your story.

YOUR SYNOPSIS SHOULD NOT:

- contain any typos (have a trusted colleague or friend proofread it);

- become caught up in plot details (capture the essence of the story rather than relaying every detail);
- include subplots (these complicate the synopsis and can confuse the reader);
- use a plethora of combined genre terms (for example: "This noir/romantic/comedy/thriller about urban senior citizens is set in the future");
- contain the phrase: "Then what happens next is . . .";
- be in screenplay format or have scene headings;
- state what the theme is;
- reveal your ending.

SYNOPSIS SAMPLE

The following is a sample synopsis. It shows the basic format to follow.

CAREER DREAMS—SAMPLE SYNOPSIS

Present day. Eva Gomez has it all. A successful career as a defense attorney for a Manhattan law firm. A loving husband. A spirited daughter with whom she shares a tight bond.

Eva embraces her fast-approaching 40th birthday while her husband, Grant Whitman, 41, lovingly teases her: "Trust me, your birthday is going to change your life dramatically." Grant plans a surprise party for Eva with their daughter, Ana, 13.

On the surface, Eva and Grant could not be more different: Eva's an overachiever dynamo from Puerto Rico and Grant, a laid-back songwriter with a cunning humor, looks the part of the *Mayflower* descendant that he is. Fifteen years of marital bliss plus Ana, a self-styled preppy who's academically and personally thriving, equals a family to envy.

One day to Eva's party. Eva suspects nothing. Ana, concerned by Grant's persistent headaches, insists they tell Eva, but Grant doesn't want to worry her. Eva's too busy with her recent promotion to partner in the law firm and considering a run for Congress. Besides, he's already seen his physician, who said it was nothing.

Dawn. Eva's birthday. Excited to start the day, Ana wakes up her mom. Together they try to wake Grant. He's not breathing. Grant was right. Eva's birthday changes her life dramatically. Grant is dead.

Three months later. Eva's investigation of Grant's death reveals medical malpractice due to his physician's misdiagnosis. Despite being an attorney, she's not interested in suing Grant's physician for monetary compensation. Money isn't going to bring back her husband. But taking action by advocating for patients' rights will honor his memory. And the most effective way to get her voice heard is to accept the bid to run for Congress.

Ana, still grief-stricken, continues to blame Eva for Grant's death. "If Dad weren't so busy with *your* birthday plans, he'd still be alive. If you weren't working all the time and ignoring us, Dad would still be alive. And if you think you're going to win that congressional seat, think again."

Although heartbroken over Ana's accusations, Eva remains driven to run for office. Their arguments escalate. Perhaps Ana is right; Eva *has* become a workaholic, and she's rarely home. Ana, hell-bent to show the world what a neglectful mother she has, cuts school, breaks curfew, and more. Eva does have it all, a full plate.

As the election draws near, Ana's behavior worsens, and she threatens to go to the press with false accusations against Eva, who is now the front-runner. Eva will not allow herself to be put in the position to choose losing Ana or the congressional seat. If only Eva can regain the once-close bond with Ana. If only they will allow themselves to heal.

WHY THIS SYNOPSIS WORKS

- It's brief, energetic, and to the point.
- It illustrates a distinct writing style.
- It uses clear, concise sentences and active verbs.
- It's written in the present tense.
- The genre is clear and consistent: Drama.
- The time period is clear: Present day.
- The setting of Manhattan is established.
- It clearly sets the stage and creates the characters' world for the reader.

- The synopsis stays focused on Eva's journey.
- It illustrates what sets this story apart: Eva's determination to run for Congress despite the obstacles she faces.
- It demonstrates Eva's distinct qualities: Resolute, an attorney, a widow, a single mother, and Puerto Rican.
- It briefly describes the main plot.
- The story arc is clear.
- It does not contain typos or scene headings.
- It doesn't get caught up in plot details or include subplots; it captures the essence of the story.
- It doesn't contain phrases like: "Then what happens next . . ."
- It doesn't state what the theme is; the theme of forgiveness is apparent.
- It clarifies the passage of time.
- It doesn't reveal the ending.

Bad Synopsis

It's always good to learn from other people's mistakes. Here is an example of what not to do when writing a synopsis. I have included all the mistakes I have read over the years as a consultant and instructor in order to show you exactly what not to do!

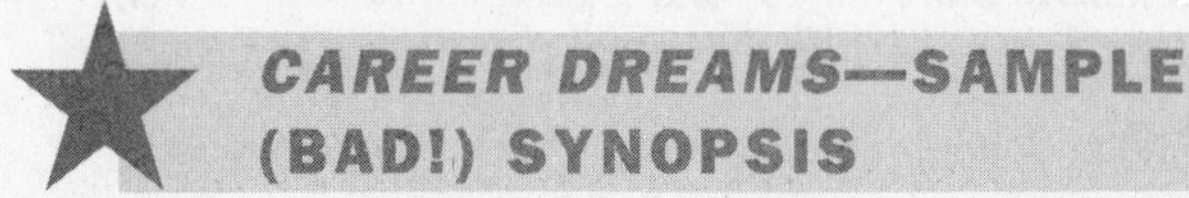

CAREER DREAMS—SAMPLE (BAD!) SYNOPSIS

Career Dreams is a drama but it's also a love story. My protagonist is a successful attorney at a law firm. She has a loving husband and spirited daughter and the family is very close. My protagonist isn't worried about turning forty soon. Her husband who turned forty a few months earlier, liked to tease her and kept telling her how this day is going to change her life dramatically. Her husband planned a surprise 40th celebration with their thirteen-year-old daughter and they have already sent out invitations to fifty family and friends and they're all coming. Husband and wife appear to be complete opposites since Eva is an overachiever who was born and raised in Puerto and her husband is a songwriter who was born and raised in Connecticut. They met as college freshmen at the University of Vermont. At first they didn't like each other but soon they fell in love. It's one day to the protagonist's party and she doesn't suspect anything. Their daughter is very worried about her father's headaches that don't stop and keeps telling him to tell her mother but he won't because she's busy working on a trial and now that she's just been made full partner in her law firm where she's worked for ten years and also her friend, Fran, who's a senator came by and think that she should run for Congress and he doesn't want to worry her. He tells his daughter that he's already seen his physician about his headaches and the physician told him it was nothing to be concerned about. It's dawn of the protagonist's birthday and the daughter is excited to start the day and she wakes up her mother. They kept trying to wake up the father but he won't wake up and he's not breathing because he's dead. After an investigation into her husband's death, the protagonist learns that his death was because of medical malpractice because his physician misdiagnosed him.

So, she decides to run for Congress. As the election gets closer and closer, the daughter's behavior gets worse and worse and she threatens her mother. This really raised the stakes in my script because the protagonist is now the front-runner in the congressional election. Meanwhile, the daughter's best friend likes the same boy she does and the two friends have a fight. And meanwhile for the mother, she is preparing to go on the local news station for a debate. Mother and daughter need to start forgiving each other and themselves for all the pain they have caused each other since the father died and this forgiveness is a major theme in my screenplay. Will mother and daughter ever reconcile? Will mother run for the senate after all? If she does run, will she win? Will the daughter renew her friendship with her best friend? Read the script and find out what happens!

WHY THIS SYNOPSIS DOES NOT WORK

- It's one long, verbose paragraph.
- Many sentences are run-ons and are not succinct.
- It doesn't state the genre, the time period, or the setting.
- It changes tenses from the present to the past and back again.
- Switching between "my protagonist," "the protagonist," and "mother" without using Eva's name further makes it impossible to follow.
- Not using the main characters' names adds to the confusion.
- Using one minor character's name, Fran, is confusing.
- It states the theme, which should not be included in

your synopsis; the theme should be evident in what you've written.

- Unnecessary details are given, such as how many invitations were sent out for the party and that husband and wife met at the University of Vermont.
- The passage of time is unclear.
- Too much time is spent on the events in Act 1.
- At the climax of the synopsis, two subplots are introduced: (1) "Meanwhile the daughter's best friend likes the same boy she does and the two friends have a fight"; and (2) "And meanwhile for the mother, she is preparing to go on the local news station for a debate." (Not only is this poorly written but it doesn't push the main plot line forward.)
- It goes from agonizing details to jumping to the mother deciding to run for Congress without explanation.
- There are confusing sentences like: "She threatens her mother" but it doesn't specify what the threat is, which could mean anything.
- Toward the end, the word "Senate" instead of "Congress" is used.
- You may want to pose a question at the end of your synopsis to further entice the reader, but be careful. Too many questions, especially questions unrelated to your main plot, are a turnoff.
- Never end your synopsis with: "Read the script and find out what happens!"

CHAPTER SEVEN

ALL ABOUT PITCHING

A pitch is exactly what it sounds like—a sales pitch. After all, this is the film *business*. A pitch can be as short as a single sentence or as long as several paragraphs, depending on what the executive has requested. Your pitch should summarize your script, entrance your listeners, emotionally move them (make them laugh! make them cry!), and convince them to spend millions of dollars turning your screenplay into a movie.

Your pitch must succinctly convey the major plot points of your story by following your unique and complex protagonist's compelling journey and story arc. Include your provocative antagonist and what's at stake in your story. Highlight the elements that distinguish your idea by verbally demonstrating how they set it apart from other films. Using descriptive images to pitch your idea will enable the listener to visualize your story. Include the genre, setting, and time period of your story.

Pitching your project presents a wonderful opportunity to establish a relationship with an executive. If you are pitching an idea about a project that you have not yet written, keep in mind: (1) once your pitch is bought, the executive/company owns it and it is theirs to do with what they want, including revising your idea to fit the company's needs; and (2) another writer may be hired to write the script based on your pitch.

Pitch ideas that you're passionate about and that you know you can translate into a solid screenplay.

WHAT TO DO WHEN YOU GET THE CALL TO PITCH

This is the moment that you've been waiting for. You receive the call that an executive wants to meet with you about your spec script. Now what? Panic? Go ahead! Get it out of your system! Then it's time to get down to work!

It's extremely challenging to nail down your entire script intelligently in just a couple of sentences, but it's crucial that you be able to do so. For examples of short pitches, read the inside flaps of book jackets, the backs of video or DVD boxes, or the summaries of the Best Picture nominees for the Academy Awards (see the "nominees" section at www.oscar.com). *TV Guide* blurbs are less accurate, and I don't recommend using those for inspiration.

Remember to register and copyright your pitch idea *prior* to your pitch meeting. At your pitch meeting bring your synopsis or treatment and include a cover page, which should have the same layout as the one in your script. The cover page should state your name, contact information, copyright symbol (©) with the year, and your WGA registration number. After your pitch, the executive may ask for your synopsis or treatment, or you may ask if you can give it to the executive. If you pitch on the phone, follow up with a letter and the material you pitched, including the cover page as noted above. If you find the opportunity to pitch in an informal chance setting (like sitting next to an executive in an airplane), ask for the person's business card and follow up with a letter and the material you pitched with the cover page as noted above. Keeping a paper trail is your best defense against the theft of your ideas.

Preparing a pitch can serve you well even if you don't have a meeting set up just yet. It will help you to hone in on your story ideas and make sure that your script is succinct. Also, when you call production companies, studios, and/or agents to learn their query submission rules, you never know who's going to pick up the telephone. There's always a good chance someone will ask, "So, what's your script about?" You should be prepared to pitch your project to them right then and there.

Don't let opportunities pass you by!

TRAPPED WITHOUT A PITCH

You never know with whom you may get stuck in an elevator. While working as an assistant in the story department at Paramount Pictures, I got stuck in an elevator for a couple of very long minutes somewhere between the thirty-first and thirty-second floor with a well-known movie star. It was my golden opportunity to pitch some of my script ideas since I had a captive audience who just asked, "You don't happen to be a screenwriter by any chance?" The answer was yes—and I had just completed a new script. But I was tongue-tied. And I didn't have a pitch prepared. What could have been a golden opportunity, even if only for practice and a way to get my mind off of being trapped in a swaying elevator, turned into a haunting and frustrating memory of a blown moment.

SEVERAL SCENARIOS TO PITCH YOUR PROJECT

- **EXECUTIVE'S, AGENT'S, OR PRODUCER'S OFFICE.** Generally you'll be given about fifteen or twenty minutes for your meeting, during which you pitch your project (and additional projects, if you're asked), leaving enough time to briefly ask and answer questions. The executive/producer/agent will let you know the length of the pitch he or she is interested in.

- **PITCH FESTIVALS.** Generally, writers are scheduled to meet for five minutes with each executive/producer/agent. Use your two-minute pitch so you'll have time for questions and feedback, and to discuss your other projects.

- **PHONE PITCH.** If you're lucky and the right person picks up the phone and you're asked to pitch, use your two-minute pitch. Never presume to pitch unless you've been asked.

- **SCREENWRITING AND FILM EVENTS.** At script conferences, film festivals, and so on, you may have the chance to network with executives, agents, producers, filmmakers, and others, which may give you the opportunity to pitch. Never presume to pitch unless you've been asked.

- **ELEVATORS, AIRPLANES, SUBWAYS, COFFEESHOPS, ANYWHERE.** You never know where the opportunity may present itself to find *captive* executives or talent, but never pitch unless it's appropriate.

FREQUENTLY ASKED QUESTIONS

If I call an agency or a production company and get their answering machine, should I pitch my project "after the tone"?

Definitely not. This is unprofessional, and the person receiving the call will press the erase button immediately.

Can I read my pitch during the meeting?

No. Your pitch must be memorized. If you think that you'll freeze up at the meeting, state in a humorous or light fashion that you have a "cheat sheet" (index cards with your written pitch) in your lap for security, and refer to them only if absolutely necessary.

At my pitch meeting, do I need to act out scenes or bring any props?

There are no set rules for pitch meetings. Writers may perform scenes or pitch their projects from their main character's point of view, bring props to illustrate the story, or stay seated and deliver a straightforward pitch. Do what best fits your personality, your ability, and your project.

Prior to your meeting, research the company to learn what the executive responds to, like genre or script styles. Reading trade publications for stories about other writers' experiences (like being cut off midsentence during a pitch) and what they did (kept pitching, walked out, threw a book) will give you some insight. Also, calling the executive's assistant may help you in uncovering some vital information.

Should I include a dialogue sample in my pitch?

If it's brief and it illustrates a character or story, then give it a try.

Do I need to prepare pitches for additional projects for my meeting?

Having more than one pitch prepared for your additional projects will be a plus. Even if the executive is not interested in the pitch that you have presented, he or she is always looking for new material.

How can I feel empowered and less at the executive's mercy at the meeting?

1. **Be prepared.** Don't use the meeting to figure out your pitch. You must be focused and not distracted.
2. **Be personable.** Make brief small talk to show that you are articulate and confident. This will convey that your project is as intelligent and as interesting as you are.
3. **Take control of the meeting.** You are the one with the great story idea and winning script. You must convey this in your meeting. Get the executive's attention. If you feel that the executive is not listening, speak slowly and quietly. The executive will sit forward in his or her seat, afraid to miss something important. If the executive is rushing the pace of the meeting, seeming impatient or speaking very quickly, you might be able to slow things down. Speak slowly, take some deep breaths, and you may set a calmer tone for the meeting.
4. **Don't be nervous.** I know, most of you are thinking, "Right, easy for *you* to say." Remember, executives

are looking for a good project and if you appear nervous, that's natural and they'll understand. Practicing your pitch prior to the meeting and knowing it inside and out will help to calm your nerves. When you're pitching your project to the executive, visualize yourself being calm and in control. Visualizing the executive in his underwear may give you the giggles!

PREPARING FOR YOUR PITCH

Prepare pitches of *approximately* two different lengths: two minutes and ten minutes. The executive/producer/agent will let you know which one to present. Usually, you will be asked to deliver a two-minute pitch, and if the person is interested in your project, then you may be asked for the longer pitch. If you're pitching your project at a pitch festival, generally you'll have five minutes per executive/producer/agent. Having a solid two-minute pitch will give you time to pitch that project, briefly discuss it, ask the person questions, and if he or she is interested, time to pitch a second project.

1. **Two-minute pitch:** State the genre, setting, and time period. Follow your unique protagonist's compelling journey and arc to illustrate your distinctive story. Include what's at stake for your protagonist and establish your captivating antagonist. Using a critical turning point in your story will help to hook the listener. Remember, your pitch should enable the listener to visualize your story.
2. **Ten-minute pitch:** In addition to adding more specific information to pitch number 1, include one

pivotal subplot and the significant minor characters and their arcs. Use the most important plot points as your guidepost.

Tips to Help You to Prepare for Your Pitch

You must keep in mind that executives are looking for an original concept and unique, complex characters that will attract talent (actors, directors, producers) to your project so it can be made into a box-office hit.

Whether your script or script idea is fiction or nonfiction, *do your research.* For example, if your script deals with medicine or law, be sure that your plot is accurate and plausible.

If you plan to compare your script to other films, choose films that were successful at the box office.

GETTING STARTED

- Visualize your idea as a film. Watch your movie in your head.
- Think about what inspired your idea, such as specific themes and major conflicts.
- How do you see the movie trailer? This can help you decide which of the major elements of your story you want to emphasize.
- Write a one-page synopsis of your story. (*See chapter 6, "Sharpening Your Synopsis."*) Then rewrite the synopsis into a pitch incorporating the tools listed below under "Content" and "The Words."
- Write an outline of your story. This will help you to further hone your ideas. Also, if you think you're going to freeze up and go blank during your pitch meeting, then bring those index cards. On your cards, highlight the major story beats and character arcs so you can quickly glance down at them if

need be. Don't read from the cards! (*See page 78 in chapter 4, "Is My Script Ready for Submission?"*)

CONTENT

- Succinctly convey your major plot points by following your unique and complex protagonist's compelling journey and story arc. Include your provocative antagonist. Use descriptive adjectives to distinguish and illustrate your characters so the listener can really grasp who they are and why he or she should care about them. Executives/producers/agents want characters with whom they and the audience can relate.
- Your protagonist's central conflict must be gripping and intriguing. The listener must know what's at stake in your story.
- Use descriptive words to clearly convey the uniqueness of your story and characters.
- Highlight the elements that distinguish your idea by verbally demonstrating how they set it apart from other films.
- Use a critical turning point in your story to hook the listener.
- State the genre.
- Briefly describe the time period and setting. Use commanding and compelling images to set the stage and create the world so the listener not only gets a solid sense of what things look like and how they feel, but can evaluate the production values.
- Know your three acts without hesitation. This doesn't necessarily mean you have to actually label each act during your pitch. Do what's appropriate for your pitch and your meeting.

THE WORDS

- Your pitch must be in the present tense; it makes the story more immediate.

- Each word must be evocative.
- Use brief but striking images to enable the listener to visualize your story.
- Use active verbs and descriptive adjectives.
- You can jump-start your pitch. For example: "According to the *Daily News*, one out of every three cops is a criminal." Then tell your story. Or you can try: "Picture this . . ." Then continue with your story. For example: "Picture this . . . a bloody, desolate Bronx street corner at midnight." (These are just examples; use whatever suits your story and makes you the most comfortable.)
- Use the names of your main characters. This personalizes the story and makes it easier to follow. To avoid confusion don't use minor characters or their names.

Rehearse Your Pitch

Your pitch meeting is like an audition—if you and your idea make a solid impression, your idea has a shot to make it to the big screen!

- Practice with timers. Focus on getting your two pitches to approximately two and ten minutes.
- Practice into a cassette and/or video recorder.
- Practice on a friend or, if possible, someone in the film industry. Have your practice audience do obnoxious things, like staring out the window or blowing bubble gum while you're pitching to them.

Research the Company You're Pitching

Know the company you're pitching to. Be sure your project and genre is appropriate for the company. Do your homework beforehand. Call ahead, read the trades, and consult the directories and resources listed in the appendix on page 257. You should learn:

- What types of projects they are looking for. This includes genres and budget ranges.
- What they have in development. You don't want to pitch a similar idea.
- What they've produced. Don't pitch a script that is similar to a box-office flop. No matter how great your script is, they're not going to want to repeat that mistake again.
- Their typical budget range. For example, you shouldn't pitch an action adventure with exotic locations to a company seeking low-budget projects.
- If they want talent attached to the project. Some companies want attachments in place prior to your meeting.
- Their sensibilities. Know the company's tastes: quirky, mainstream, and so on.
- Their development process. This includes their expectations for the writers with whom they work.

SEIZE YOUR PITCH MEETING

A pitch meeting is essentially a job interview. Be punctual. Appear professional. Be articulate about yourself and your project. Thank them for taking the time to meet with you. Your confidence must be apparent in how you present yourself, not to mention your work!

TIPS TO GRAB EXECUTIVES' ATTENTION

- You're selling, not only your story, but yourself. If you are pitching an idea for a script not yet written, you must prove to them that you are the best candidate to write it. If you are pitching a script that you've already written, your pitch must entice them to request a copy.

- Remember, a script takes ninety minutes or longer to read, and you have two minutes to pitch and make a great impression.
- Be excited and passionate about your project. If you're not, they won't be.
- Engage the executives. For example, if you're pitching a comedy, your goal is to make them laugh.
- Stay focused!
- Bring your résumé and a synopsis, treatment, and/or script with you in case they ask for them.
- At the end of your pitch, ask them if they have any questions.
- After your meeting, drop the executive a thank-you note. You've just made an industry connection, and you want to keep it!

PITCHING DON'TS

- Don't say: "I'm passionate about my idea!" Your passion must come through in your pitch.
- Listeners want to hear just what your story is *about*; they don't want to hear the whole story.
- Don't recite your pitch scene by scene and/or act by act; you'll put them to sleep.
- Don't tell the listener what the character arc is; it should be evident in your pitch. If the person is interested in learning more about specific characters, he or she will ask you. This opens the door for you to go into more detail.
- Don't waste your listener's time by rambling on with unnecessary details about your story or chatter about your personal life; quickly get to the point.

The Yawn

INT. MAJOR STUDIO OFFICE - DAY

A slick and modern office. Susan, now 25, enters confidently, dressed in a stylish suit.

EXECUTIVE, 21, hip and cocky, CHATS on his cell phone with his feet on his empty and spotless desk. He manages a phony smile without making eye contact and motions for Susan to sit.

Susan takes a seat and waits.

SUSAN (V.O.)

I sat and waited for this pitch meeting to start. And waited. And waited. And waited. I tried not to show it, but my confidence was dwindling.

Executive finally hangs up. And yawns. And yawns. And yawns.

SUSAN (V.O.) (CONT'D)

I knew that I had to take the initiative and seize control of this meeting.

Susan leans forward in her chair and looks directly at Executive. His attention is on his manicured fingernails.

SUSAN (CONT'D)

Worked late last night?

EXECUTIVE

No. (yawn) Lunch.

SUSAN

Lunch?

EXECUTIVE

Had . . . (yawn) a big . . . (yawn) . . . lunch. (yawn) Sorry.

SUSAN

(testing the boundaries)

Liquid lunch?

Finally, Executive makes eye contact.

EXECUTIVE

(perks up)

If only.

MONTAGE

Dramatic symphonic MUSIC builds to a climax during Montage.

--Susan calmly and semiconfidently presents her first pitch.

--Executive stares at the floor and unsuccessfully fights yet another yawn.

--Susan presents her second pitch. She looks more confident as she gestures wildly with enthusiasm.

--Executive sits at the edge of his seat, engrossed. He's almost out of breath with excitement. No more yawns.

END MONTAGE

EXECUTIVE

Here's the deal. Hated the first pitch. Loved the second. Let me call your agent while I've got you here to get that script.

Executive dials her agent's number.

SUSAN (V.O.)

I was thrilled by his response, but so drained by the experience that I could barely contain my--

Susan lets out a huge yawn.

PSYCHOANALYZING MOVIE EXECUTIVES

Movie executives have reputations for being intimidating and tough. We've all seen them portrayed in movies as nothing less than monsters, and we have read in magazines and the industry trades about some of their unscrupulous ways. Don't let these portrayals and stories overwhelm you. Movie executives are people, too, and most don't fit the stereotypes.

- Put yourself in their positions. Their jobs are on the line. You don't know how many pitches they've heard that day. It's not easy being on the receiving end.
- Executives are trained not to react. Even if they love your pitch, they may stare at the floor or tap on the desk, so it's hard to get an accurate reading.
- Executives are eager to discover a new hit, yet at the same time they're conservative and not too willing to part with the company's money.
- Executives know their craft, and they know what they are looking for. Your project must fit into their marketing schemes, and they must be able to sell your pitch to their bosses.
- The executive is essentially hiring you as the representative to get the financing for your joint project. Look at it this way—your great pitch helps both of you.

WHAT TO EXPECT AT YOUR MEETING

- You don't know how much time you have. You may get caught short. Phones may ring or someone will pop into the office. Don't get flustered!
- Direct your pitch to everyone in the room. If someone walks in during your pitch, include him or her in your pitch as well.

- You might hear: "The part of the pitch that I'm uncomfortable with . . ." Or: "The part of the pitch that doesn't work for me . . ." Or: "Where I lost interest was . . ." Take such comments seriously. You may have had a weak character or a contrived story element. Don't go on the defensive! Thank them and take mental notes on this feedback.
- There is no going back once you hear: "I can't sell it." Don't argue; the executive knows what his or her company is looking for.
- If the executive has passed on your first pitch idea, there's no harm in asking if you can pitch another project.
- If the executive likes your basic idea, he or she may present you with story ideas to help you to modify the script to meet the company's needs. Take note of their ideas and feedback.
- The executive is anxious to grasp what your pitch is about. He or she may ask: "Do the main characters fall in love or not?" Answer the question; don't be cagey.
- The executive may not buy the idea that you're pitching but may give you the opportunity to pitch another script idea, which could be just what they're looking for.
- If your meeting goes well, ask if you can come back with additional pitch ideas in the future.

QUESTIONS YOU MAY BE ASKED AT YOUR PITCH MEETING

- Who is your audience? (Meaning: art house, youth, mainstream, and so on.)
- What other films would you compare this to? (Be sure that your comparisons are to successful box-office films.)
- What drew you to this material? (Meaning: A personal experience, an article you read, and so on.)

- Who are the secondary characters? What is the subplot? (Be sure that your response provides a clear insight.)
- What do you estimate the budget being? (They're not asking you to give an exact figure. Stating low, medium, or high is sufficient.)
- Do you have any talent (actors, producers, or director) attached to the project?
- Which actors do you see in the major roles? (They're not asking you to cast the film; they're just trying to get an idea of what's in your head.)
- Have other companies, producers, and/or talent expressed interest in the project you've just pitched? (Respond honestly. Remember, in the film industry everyone knows everyone else; and if they don't, they know someone who does.)

THE BADGE IS ON THE OTHER CHEST

Years ago, two of my short films were shown at the Independent Feature Film Market (IFFM) in New York City. I remember the nerve-racking wait among the crowd of other screenwriters and filmmakers to meet executives. When I finally got my chance, I asked them if it was okay to pitch my project. It was all very civilized.

A few years later I found myself on the other side. I was a buyer for Warner Bros. seeking acquisitions and directing talent at the IFFM. I was given the green buyer's ID badge. I saw it as a badge. Screenwriters and filmmakers saw it as a target. I soon learned that "green" means "go," as in attack. Literally.

Filmmakers and screenwriters zeroed in on me—they pointed at my green badge and shouted phrases from their pitches in desperate attempts to snare my attention. I understood their anguish as they fought through a crowd of other filmmakers and screenwriters clamoring for attention from executives and agents—and knowing that this could be their one shot at making contact.

The surge of screenwriters and filmmakers fell into three groups: the underconfident, the misguided, and the overconfident.

The underconfident filmmakers/screenwriters

They would open their pitches with a whole string of apologies seemingly designed to provide me with every excuse I needed *not* to see their film or read their script. They'd say: "I know that you're not interested in my film or my script, and you probably don't have time and it's not really finished, and I'm not really sure I like it anyhow, but maybe you'll want to come to my screening or read my script." I'd think, no, I'll go get a cup of coffee instead.

The misguided filmmakers/screenwriters

They would zero in on my green badge and grab their opportunity—launching into a long and involved pitch without asking me if I would like to hear it. They would keep talking and talking despite the fact that I'd made it clear from their first words that theirs was not a project that Warner Bros. would ever consider. It became embarrassing, like being the subject of a case of mistaken identity.

Maybe I was too polite. I should have firmly interrupted them and said, "You've got the wrong person.

Don't waste your time or my time pitching to me. You should be pitching to that person over there who can really help you. And, in the future, ask executives if they are interested in hearing a pitch. If they say yes, make it brief and exciting."

The overconfident filmmakers/screenwriters

I walked in the door, anxious to get to a screening on time. The usual surge of screenwriters and filmmakers approached me—pressing flyers on me, inviting me to their screenings, shouting and interrupting each other in their clamor for my attention. Understanding their frenzy, I tried to stop for each one on my way to the screening room. One guy certainly made a lasting impression as I was listening to another filmmaker's pitch. He stepped between us, pushed my hair away from where it accidentally was covering my green ID badge and shouted at me that I should be more accessible. I will always remember him, but not in the way he wanted me to.

I was even followed into the ladies' room by an eager female filmmaker who kept pitching after I had politely but firmly closed the stall door. I later learned that, by virtue of my gender, I was among the lucky ones. A less-fortunate male buyer told me of an encounter he had at the urinal. As he zipped up his fly, a filmmaker approached him and impulsively asked, "Are you interested in shorts?"

There are definitely right and wrong places and times to pitch.

CHAPTER EIGHT

THE RED CARPET TREATMENT

WHAT EXACTLY IS A TREATMENT?

A treatment is a detailed overview of a screenplay or script idea written in prose form that is used as a marketing tool for both spec and for-hire screenwriters to sell their project. It can be considered a written pitch.

Producers, studios, and/or production companies usually request treatments *after* you pitch a project idea to them. They will then tell you how many pages to make your treatment. The average length of a treatment is usually between ten and thirty pages, but a treatment can also be as short as one page.

Executives and producers use treatments as both a selling tool to get your movie made and as a way to identify story, characters, and structural strengths and weaknesses.

Executives, producers, and companies have enormous amounts of material to plow through, so reading a treatment as opposed to a screenplay takes less time. Keep in mind that if you write a treatment for the purpose of pitching it to a company without writing the script, it may lessen your chances of being hired.

It's not really necessary to write a treatment along with your spec script unless it assists you in the writing process. Many writers write treatments solely for their own purposes and, like an executive, use their treatments to determine the story's strengths and weaknesses.

A treatment that is written for submission to a company must clearly reflect your talent as a writer. Executives are looking for unique and marketable subject matter that an audience can relate to so they can sell it!

Treatments are evaluated on several levels. Is this a good, marketable story? Does the writer have the talent and ability to translate this into a great screenplay? Whether you write a treatment based on your original idea, an adaptation of a novel, or a true story, the reader will evaluate your ability to dramatize your work into a riveting story complete with captivating characters and a solid structure.

Like a screenplay, your treatment must immediately grab the reader's attention. It must have energy! The reader must get a vivid sense of your story: what it looks like and how it feels. Use visual imagery to describe your settings and time periods. Distinguish your characters so the reader has a clear understanding of who they are (such as profession or personality) and what motivates their actions.

Your treatment must illustrate the hook of your story. The readers' standard questions are: "What sets your story apart from others about the same subject? What makes both your story and your approach unique?"

Your story must continue to build momentum from page one line, one right, through to the very last sentence. Your treatment must feel immediate to the reader; each event about to unfold must create interest and excitement.

Your treatment must highlight the broad strokes of your

story, your main characters, and your turning points. Follow your protagonist's journey in sequential order, from beginning to end. Clearly describe your characters and their arcs, their motivations for their actions, and the obstacles they must overcome. The story's point of view must be clear so the reader knows whose story you're telling.

As opposed to a screenplay, there is no specific industry format for a treatment. However, there are some basic guidelines to follow:

- Write your treatment in block paragraph form, that is, without using indentations and skipping a space between paragraphs.
- Suggested fonts are: Courier New 12 or Times New Roman 12.
- Use separate ACT 1, ACT 2, and ACT 3 headings to delineate each act.
- Use quotation marks for dialogue.

YOUR TREATMENT SHOULD:

- excite the reader to want to read your screenplay;
- be a clear and accurate reflection of your screenplay (if you've already written it);
- illustrate your hook—what makes this different from other stories about the same subject matter;
- be easy, interesting, and enjoyable to read;
- contain short rather than long paragraphs;
- be written in visual prose;
- be written in the present tense;
- have precise and simple sentences, since each word counts;
- have a strong opening to hook the reader;

- have a compelling and satisfying climax;
- have a clear structure;
- establish what's at stake in your story;
- have an intriguing and empathetic protagonist the reader will root for;
- follow your protagonist's journey and arc;
- include the central conflict and obstacles your protagonist must overcome;
- establish your antagonist and his or her goals;
- include the main and supporting characters;
- include the major plot points and turning points;
- illustrate action and description;
- include minimal or no back story;
- include snippets of dialogue, using quotation marks, but only to illustrate a poignant or critical moment that further defines the character and/or story.

YOUR TREATMENT SHOULD NOT:

- use screenplay format;
- use flowery language;
- include unnecessary details;
- include author's editorial comments;
- include characters' inner thoughts;
- include phrases like "It's a story about . . ." or "What happens next is . . ." Just tell the story.

TREATMENT SAMPLE

The following is a sample treatment. It shows the basic format to follow.

CAREER DREAMS—SAMPLE TREATMENT FOR ACT 1.

ACT 1

Eva Gomez has it all. A successful career as a defense attorney for a Manhattan law firm. A loving husband. A spirited daughter with whom she shares a tight bond.

An ominous late winter snowstorm in SoHo. Golf ball-sized hail strikes the windows of a trendy restaurant, where Eva and her husband, Grant Whitman, and their daughter Ana, 13, celebrate Eva's promotion to partner in her law firm.

On the surface, Eva and Grant could not be more different. An overachiever from Puerto Rico, Eva, a dynamo, is distinctly attractive with her long black hair and dark complexion. Grant, a laid-back songwriter with a cunning humor, looks like the blonde, fair-skinned *Mayflower* descendant that he is. Fifteen years of a happy marriage plus Ana, a self-styled preppy who's thriving academically and personally, equals a family to envy.

Eva embraces her fast-approaching 40th birthday while Grant, 41, lovingly teases her: "Trust me, your birthday is going to change your life dramatically." Ana giggles as her parents kiss. A hail ball smashes through the restaurant window, nearly striking Eva.

At their modest yet cozy Brooklyn living room, Grant and Ana make their final arrangements for Eva's surprise 40th birthday party while Eva does her legal work in the study.

Eva's no-nonsense friend, State Senator Fran Bloom, drops by with news: the congressional seat in their district has been vacated. Fran begs Eva to run for his seat. Eva quickly dismisses her; it would leave little time with her family. Grant's openly gung ho while Ana hides her reticence.

One day to Eva's surprise party. Eva suspects nothing. Ana, concerned by Grant's persistent headaches, insists they tell Eva. Grant doesn't want to worry Eva: she's busy with a trial and working with Fran on the bid for Congress. Besides, he's already seen his physician, who said it was nothing.

Dawn. Eva's birthday. Excited to start the day, Ana wakes up her mom. Together they try to wake Grant. He won't wake up. He's not breathing. Ana calls 911 as Eva tries to resuscitate him. An ambulance speeds Grant to the local hospital with Eva and Ana at his side. But it's too late. Grant is dead.

Grief-stricken, Ana blames Eva for Grant's death. "If Dad weren't so busy with *your* birthday plans, if you weren't working all the time and ignoring us, Dad would still be alive. And if you think you're going to win that congressional seat, think again."

WHY THIS TREATMENT SAMPLE WORKS

- It's an easy read.
- It's written in the present tense, with precise and simple sentences in visual prose and short paragraphs.
- It has a clear structure.

- The main characters, Eva, Grant, and Ana, are briefly described in order for the reader to get a visual picture of them.
- The hook establishes Grant's death and Eva's new single motherhood with a grief-stricken daughter, as well as the possibility of Eva's running for Congress.
- The stakes in the story are established: mother/daughter conflict over Grant's death and Eva's congressional run.
- Eva is an intriguing and empathetic protagonist the reader will root for.
- It follows Eva's journey and arc.
- It includes the central conflict and obstacles the protagonist, Eva, must overcome by showing Ana blaming Eva for Grant's death.
- Ana's character shifts from loving daughter to the antagonist at the turning point of Act 1.
- We meet the main characters (Eva and Ana) and supporting characters, Grant and Fran.
- The major plot and turning points are clearly established.
- The actions are clearly described.
- There is minimal backstory.
- Snippets of dialogue with quotation marks are used to illustrate a poignant and critical moment that further defines the character and story.
- It does not include unnecessary details and flowery language or contain editorial comments or characters' inner thoughts. Phrases like "It's a story about . . ." and "What happens next is . . ." are not used.

YOUR DREAM SCENARIO WHEN YOU SUBMIT YOUR TREATMENT

You've done an impressive job pitching your story idea to a company, and they request your treatment. (Of course, you register your treatment with the WGA and copyright it prior to submitting it, and the cover page of your treatment will include this information.) You or your agent, manager, or entertainment attorney submits your brilliant treatment to a company.

The development executive reads your treatment, loves your writing and your story, and requests your screenplay. A story analyst reads your screenplay and writes positive coverage. The development executive pitches your idea to his or her boss who could be the head of development, company head, or other executive).

The boss is thrilled and you are invited to meet with the company executives. You make a very good impression because you are articulate, express yourself confidently, and are open to their feedback.

They really like you, and you really like them. They want to make a deal. You like them even more!

Your agent or lawyer negotiates their offer because you know that it's imperative to have professional representation. The deal is negotiated to everyone's satisfaction. You go out and celebrate . . . and keep writing!

CHAPTER NINE

OKAY, I FINALLY FINISHED MY SCRIPT, QUERY, SYNOPSIS, PITCH, AND TREATMENT . . . NOW WHAT?

Congratulations! Take yourself out to dinner and a movie. Better yet, have a friend or loved one take you out to dinner and a movie. Then take a day off and rest because your work is about to continue.

PUT ON YOUR PRODUCER'S CAP

The task of getting your script read might seem overwhelming at first and at second and at third, but there is a method to the madness. The secret is to act as your own producer.

You are the best person to represent your script. Even if you have an agent, your agent has other clients, and you will still have to do the legwork. You have labored over and lived with your script for months, maybe years. Don't take any chances.

RESEARCH

1. **Use an up-to-date resource directory.** Remember, development executives come and go, so

someone who's working at a company today may be gone tomorrow. *(See the appendix on page 257.)*

2. **Research companies producing in your genre.**
   - Learn the company's submission rules and find out what they're looking for. For example: Querying a major studio or big packaging agency with an experimental narrative art-house script, or querying a boutique agency or an independent producer with limited financial resources with an action script will most likely be the wrong choice.
   - Be sure that your project is appropriate for the studio or production company in terms of budget range.
   - Find out if the company expects financing or talent to be attached to your project.
   - Learn what other projects the company has produced, either by calling them or researching the trade publications and other resources. *(See the appendix on page 257.)*
   - If the company is new and has no credits, ask for references. If none are forthcoming, you do not want to work with this company.
   - If a company requires a reading fee, do not send your script.
3. **Read the trades.** *Variety* and *The Hollywood Reporter,* for example, list films in preproduction and development. These and other resources list spec script sales and who buys what. *(See the appendix on page 257.)*
4. **Go to the video store.** Peruse the New Release section. Read the back of DVD and video boxes to determine which studio or production companies

produced the projects in your genre. Call these companies and ask what types of projects they are currently seeking. Also, contact the producers or directors with query letters.

5. **Go to the movies.** See the films in the genre that you're working in. Contact the producers and directors with query letters.

TARGETING COMPANIES: THE HIT LIST

Know Who to Include on your Hit List

Many new writers target only the major studios. Don't limit yourself. Numerous independent production companies produce quality films. Additionally, cable networks like HBO, Showtime, and Lifetime are producing high-caliber projects.

Target Talent

"Getting talent attached" means that you have gotten interest from a director, actor(s), or producer(s) to work on your project. While a letter of interest from talent does not ensure a firm commitment, it will spark the interest of companies.

This may seem like an arduous process, but start by asking people you know for contacts. You never know where this may lead. If you don't have any personal contacts and you are looking to query actors or directors, go to the SAG (Screen Actors Guild) or the DGA (Directors Guild of America) Web sites to find the names of their agents or managers and send your query letters to those people. You can also check the Internet Movie Database (www.imdb.com) to learn who produced the actor's last films. This actor may also have his or her own production company. *(See the appendix on page 257 for more listings.)*

Be aware that most agents and managers will shield their clients from first timers because they want their clients to make money. Often they will consider a project for their client only if there is financing already in place.

Target Smaller Production Companies

Many smaller production companies have studio deals that give them offices on studio lots. Some of these companies are looking for and are open to working with new writers.

A small production company will have a small staff consisting of: the producer (owner of the company), the producer's assistant, the president or executive vice president (an experienced executive who may bring in new material and/or help to run the company), and his or her assistant. There may be one or two additional executives with titles such as vice president and/or director of development (most companies have both), and they may have assistants.

One of these aforementioned assistants may also work as the company's story editor, so he or she will oversee all submitted material. These companies receive scripts from agents and managers whom they trust and who know their sensibilities. The story editor will either do the script coverage personally or assign it to an in-house or freelance story analyst.

Remember, today's assistant is tomorrow's executive. This is the person with whom you want to develop a relationship. Assistants are establishing themselves in the industry, and they're looking for new talent to help advance their own careers. Assistants have the producer's attention. If the assistant likes your work, his or her boss will read it.

Develop a Hit List

It's vital to keep track of the names of your contacts as well as the dates you sent out your material and the responses that you received. Your hit list should include:

1. Companies' names: mailing, e-mail, and Web addresses; phone and fax numbers; along with their pertinent information.
2. The names of people contacted, when and what material you sent (logline, query, synopsis, and/or script), and to whom the material was sent. (If you pitched your project on the phone or in person, note the name, contact information, and response.)
3. Any vital (or just very interesting) information about those contacts.
4. The company's response to your material: favorable or pass.
5. Note when to follow up with material or a phone call, an e-mail, or a letter.
6. A record of your expenses.

DON'T GET TOO ANXIOUS OR MAKE BLUNDERS

Don't start sending out your script to everyone on your hit list until it has been requested. Agencies, production companies, and studios are inundated with scripts daily, if not hourly. Sending a script without its being requested is unacceptable business etiquette and a sure guarantee that it will be thrown into the circular file. If you don't have an agent, you may be asked to sign a release form. This is a legal document that protects production companies and studios from charges of theft of ideas. *(See chapter 1, "Your Questions—My Answers.")*

YOUR "PRODUCER'S CAP" CHECKLIST

- Call the agent and/or company on your hit list to confirm the proper spelling and title of the executive you are querying and to ask for their submission guidelines.
- Be prepared with your pitch in the event that an assistant or executive on the other end of the phone line asks you what your script is about.
- If the assistant or executive requests your synopsis and/or script, include a cover letter with your contact information and thank them for their interest.
- If you don't have the opportunity to pitch your project on the telephone, mail your query with an SASE.
- Take a lot of deep breaths and wait patiently for a response. It may be anywhere from two to six weeks or more until you hear from the company.

HURRY UP AND WAIT

Life couldn't be better! You have just received a response letter in your SASE—or you have just received a phone call from the film executive or agent you queried. The company is interested in your project and has just asked you to send your script to them—immediately.

You write a brilliant cover letter, and you double-check to make sure your script is clean and all the pages are there and in order. You run to the post office and make it inside just as they are locking the doors. You overnight your script. You do your own private good-luck ritual dance. Then weeks pass and you don't hear a word from the executive. This appears to be the nature of the business: a frantic frenzy to get your script to the executive, and then the long wait. You are not alone. (I've been there. I'm still there. I've even considered writing a theme song titled "Hurry Up and Wait.")

It is absolutely acceptable to call or write the agent and/or company to find out the status of your script. You may find that a story analyst has not yet evaluated your script, or that it never arrived at the right department, or that it did arrive but the executive or agent who requested your script is no longer working there. Usually, your script will have arrived, but checking in will be a positive and gentle reminder that you are awaiting a response.

DON'T BE TOO HUNGRY

Don't rush into a relationship with the first person who expresses interest in your work. If an agent or company is interested in you, then you must find out about them.

COMMON SENSE

When I first got into the film business, I uncharacteristically lost my common sense. I didn't trust my rational gut instincts. Why? I wanted to write. I wanted to see my scripts made into films. If someone had asked me to jump, I would have asked not only, "How high?" but also, "For how long?" Whether dealing with an independent production company, a studio, or agent, I was putty in their hands.

I didn't ask questions. I didn't ask producers if they had financing or talent in place, what projects they'd produced in the past, or what projects they currently had in development. (One fledgling company that lacked credits and financing but talked a convincing game hired me for a rewrite assignment. I was so excited that I didn't trust my gut instincts about these so-called producers. More important, I didn't have an attorney read my contract before I signed on the dotted line. So, after all my hard work, I didn't get paid when the company went bust.) I didn't ask agents how they planned on working with me or how they thought they could sell my work. (I was represented by agents who wanted me as part of their stable of writers, but they didn't really know how to place my work. Because I never asked what type of scripts they actually sold, or if any of my scripts might be submitted as writing samples to companies, or if I should write another script in a different genre to show my diversity, or offered suggestions as to where to submit my scripts, I never got hired for assignments and didn't sell one script.) By not asking questions, I often worked with people who didn't share my vision of my work or career. If you don't ask questions, you might just repeat my mistakes!

NETWORKING KNOW-HOW

You've heard that it's all about who you know. And it's true. You must create your own opportunities. There are no shortcuts. Meet people. Make a great impression. And never burn bridges.

The following tips will help you to become savvier:

1. **Be brave.** Even your most obscure connections to actors, directors, producers, and so on may be a lead. If your neighbor's cousin's sister-in-law is an assistant

at a studio and suggests you send a query, do so. Don't be shy. Everyone is looking for a good script.

2. **Find work in a film-related field.** Intern, volunteer, or temp at a studio, a production company, an agency, a writers' or film organization, a film festival, a pitch festival, and/or a script conference. Even working in some capacity on a student film may open future doors.
3. **Take classes.** Take writing, directing, and/or acting classes with instructors who are in the film industry. If you don't live in an area where these classes are offered, or you have scheduling conflicts, join online screenwriting classes.
4. **Join writers' groups.** This is a great way to have your work read by others—to get feedback as well as to share resources, stories, and insights about the film business.
5. **Message boards.** Many screenwriting and filmmaking Web sites provide message boards. This is a good way to learn from screenwriters' and filmmakers' experiences and get information about script competitions, agents, and potential leads to producers and production companies.
6. **Have a script reading.** Setting up an informal or formal reading is a great chance for both you and others to hear your work. It's also an opportunity for you to invite agents and film executives (or people who might know them) as a way to get you and your work noticed.
7. **Attend script readings.** This is a good opportunity to meet other screenwriters, support and hear their work, and learn from their experiences.

8. **Attend film and pitch festivals, film and script markets, seminars, and writers' conferences.** Aside from learning more about the writing process and the film industry, this is a savvy way to share information with other writers and to meet industry professionals.

NAVIGATING YOUR WAY THROUGH SCRIPT AND FILM MARKETS, FILM AND PITCH FESTIVALS, AND CONFERENCES

There are many annual events that give you the chance to meet executives face-to-face and develop relationships.

At several of these events, screenwriters (usually for a fee) can have their scripts listed in the event catalogue and/or placed in a library that organizers set up only for the duration of the event.

During this time, interested companies can read your script or they may request your script after the event is over.

I have been on both sides of these events—as a screenwriter/filmmaker and as an executive seeking material. It can be daunting trying to get executives' attention. Why? There may be hundreds of screenwriters in the room who want to meet the same executives that you have on your hit list. You may be elbowing for space in a mob trying to meet them. Some executives may seem elusive and unavailable. They're very busy and have their own jobs to do. Don't take it personally.

It's important to note that if you have a script in an event library, chances are that the executives will not take the time to read your script there. (It's unlikely that they have two spare minutes, let alone hours, to read anything.) If you're lucky, they may take a quick glance at it. This doesn't mean that the executive isn't interested in your work. It just means that they don't have the time.

BUYER BRUSH-OFF

When I worked as a buyer seeking acquisitions and directing talent for Warner Bros. and Republic Pictures at several Independent Feature Film Markets, eager screenwriters and filmmakers inundated me, vying for my attention. *(See "The Badge Is on the Other Chest" on page 160.)* I knew firsthand (because I was in the same boat) how important it was for them to make personal connections with me—a studio consultant by day—and an independent filmmaker and screenwriter by night. I tried my best to meet with everyone, listen to pitches, and answer questions. I also tried my best to tell them that my time was limited (but too often my pleas for understanding fell on desperate, deaf ears). I wasn't brushing anyone off. Each day my bosses gave me a list of films I had to see and report on. My time was not my own. I had specific assignments and daily deadlines. I could not be late for or miss a screening.

So the next time you approach executives who may appear to be brushing you off, just remember that they might have assignments and deadlines to meet.

Before, During, and After the Event Tips

BEFORE THE EVENT

Create an announcement. Compose a one-page flyer or postcard. Do what suits your budget. Your announcement should contain the following:

1. A great pitch. Describe your project in one or two attention-grabbing sentences.
2. A very brief bio highlighting your most important credits.
3. Your contact information while at the event. You can print this information on a sticker so you can use your announcement for other purposes.
4. Your home or office contact information. Include: address, phone and fax numbers, and e-mail, if you have it.
5. You can include an eye-catching graphic, but the content is the most important.
6. Send your announcement to the executives you are interested in targeting. Snail mail is preferable. Faxes tend to be ignored. Although e-mails can be easily deleted and quickly forgotten, sending both an e-mail and mailing a hard copy of your announcement is a good option.

DURING THE EVENT

1. When meeting an executive be brief and polite. Introduce yourself, state that you have a project at the event, and give them your announcement.

Remember that it's the executive's turn to make the next move.

2. Don't stalk the executive. *(See "The Badge Is on the Other Chest" on page 160.)*
3. Don't pitch your project to an executive unless you are asked to. *(See "The Badge Is on the Other Chest" on page 160.)*
4. Don't hand an executive a script unless it is requested. Generally, if the executive is interested, you will be asked to send it.
5. If executives have mailboxes at the event, putting your announcement in mailboxes is acceptable unless the event guidelines state otherwise.
6. Never stuff a script that has not been requested into an executive's mailbox.
7. Don't put query letters into mailboxes. This is seen as unprofessional, and generally your letter will be quickly thrown away. Query letters should be mailed to an executive unless otherwise requested.
8. Exchange business cards with executives. After the meeting be sure to write a note to yourself on the back of the card to remind you of your conversation. (Trust me, once the event is over it's unlikely that you'll recall exactly what was said to whom.)
9. If you find yourself dozing off during a panelist's talk, then leave the room. Panelists will take note of sleeping participants.

OOOPS! THE SPOTLIGHT IS NOW ON YOU!

I know it can be exhausting attending seminars, particularly if you're sneaking time from your job to attend. However, nodding off while a panelist is speaking is rude and can cause you great embarrassment.

I've spoken on panels, seated alongside my colleagues, when an attendee has fallen asleep. It's usually one of the attendees who has asked his or her questions, is satisfied with the response, and then decides to catch a few *zzzz*'s—perhaps in the hope that pearls of wisdom will filter in through his or her dreams. This unsuspecting snoozer may think he or she won't be noticed in a crowd of enthusiastic screenwriters. But take note: my fellow panelists and I are watching. And each time this has happened, a fellow panelist has directly asked the sleeper a question. When the sleeper doesn't respond, the panelist will then say something embarrassing, which in turn causes the audience to laugh so loud it wakes the sleeping beauty—whose eyelids slowly open to the eyes of the audience and the panelists. This is obviously not the way to grab industry professionals' attention.

AFTER THE EVENT

1. Follow up with an "It was nice to meet you" letter. If you didn't have the opportunity to meet the targeted executive, send a letter introducing yourself and your project; state that you attended that event and regret

not having had the opportunity to meet. You can enclose your project's announcement with this letter. (Sending a letter rather than an e-mail is preferable.)

2. Now, try to relax . . . if you can!

PITCH FESTIVALS

More and more pitch festivals have emerged over the last few years. Choose the festival or festivals that best suits your specific needs. Do your research! Most festivals offer screenwriters several pitch opportunities with various agents, producers, and/or executives. Usually there is a separate fee per pitch, so in order to use this opportunity to your best advantage, find out how many pitches you can sign up for, what they charge, and if and how you can select the person you want to pitch to.

When researching the pitch festivals, learn which companies, agents, and executives will be listening to pitches, the types of projects they've been involved with in the past, and what they're looking for now. *(See the appendix on page 257.)*

Generally, you're given about five or ten minutes to pitch your project in person to an industry professional. The pressure is on you, so be prepared with a solid pitch prior to the festival. (*See chapter 7, "All About Pitching."*)

I hate to sound pessimistic, but the likelihood of pitching your project in five or ten minutes and clinching a sale on the spot is a long shot. But don't let this discourage you. This is your chance to sit down face-to-face with industry professionals. Use this golden opportunity to make personal connections and follow up with them after the festival. This is how business relationships are established.

Most agents, executives, and producers who attend pitch festivals are looking for new material and to discover new talent. Many really do want to help you, so take this opportunity to ask for their feedback on your pitch. Also, ask what genres they're looking for and what they currently have in development. Keep notes on each meeting.

Remember, you're selling yourself, not only your pitch. Producers, executives, and agents seek writers who can deliver a great script. You must make a good impression. Be articulate. Respect the person to whom you are pitching.

SCRIPT COMPETITIONS

Winning a competition is another way to get your foot in the door. Listings for script competitions can be found in most film and screenwriting magazines, as well as online film and screenwriting Web sites. (*See the appendix on page 257.*)

Competition winners are often listed in trade publications, and this will certainly grab the industry's attention. Having a winning credit attached to your script will give you the needed edge over the competition.

CURATOR CALLING

Soon after I won first place at a short-film festival, a film curator at the Museum of Modern Art in New York (who was one of the festival's judges) contacted me to acquire that short film for the museum's permanent collection. This acquisition led to a long-term relationship with MoMA. Several years later, MoMA requested all six of my short films for their archives. Having the MoMA stamp of approval opened countless doors to film industry connections, agents, and other film festivals.

Additionally, placing as a finalist in several prestigious screenwriting competitions helped tremendously in getting my scripts to the targeted names on my hit list of companies and talent.

There are hundreds of script competitions to choose from that offer a variety of enticements to attract screenwriters. Some screenwriters who have won competitions have received positive attention, which helped to launch their careers, while other winners have received little or no attention from winning.

Some competitions' sponsors may be well-known producers, actors, directors, and/or executives. Don't confuse or make the assumption that a sponsor is going to actually be a judge. Read the competition's guidelines and promotion materials very carefully and note exactly who the judges are.

Some competitions state that the top prize is agent representation. This may be legitimate, but keep in mind that even if you win and get agent representation, it doesn't ensure the fact that the agent will enthusiastically promote your work.

Submitting your work to script competitions can be expensive and time-consuming, so you must do your research. There are numerous print and online publications that list contests and articles about the good, bad, and ugly script competitions. (*See the appendix on page 257.*) The more specific information the competition provides, the better; so carefully read and follow the contest guidelines.

SCRIPT COMPETITION POINTERS

1. Read the fine print. Carefully read and precisely follow the instructions and requirements for each competition, as they differ.

2. Target competitions that pertain to your genre, subject matter, and/or your personal background: age, ethnicity, where you live, and occupation.
3. Make sure the competition is legitimate and find out:
   - Who is sponsoring it? For example, are they backed by a studio, film organization, or trade publication? The people or entity sponsoring the competition must have film industry credentials.
   - Who are the judges? You want at least one judge to be an industry name.
   - How long has the competition been in existence? Submitting work to an event that has been around for several years and is respected by the industry is a better choice.
   - Do they list past competition winners? Researching previous winners to see how they fared after the competition is always helpful.
   - Aside from a cash prize, what other incentives are they offering? For example: Will they announce winners in trade publications, send out press releases, or submit the winning script to name agents or companies? Do they offer a staged reading of the winning script? Do they offer all-expense-paid trips to New York City and/or Hollywood for meetings with industry professionals? Any of these examples are good incentives to enter the competition. However, make sure that these are legitimate offers.
   - If the contest promises that the winner's script will be produced, that's great, but ask them for the previous winner's e-mail address to learn more about their experience.

TIPS FOR ENTERING SCRIPT COMPETITIONS

- Enter early. Scripts that are entered early are often read early, which means that the reader may not gloss over your work.
- Fill out forms legibly. It sounds obvious, but you'd be surprised at the messy forms that are submitted. Don't risk rejection due to sloppiness.
- Don't invent genres. Be professional, not clever.
- Include the appropriate contest fee. Paper clip it to the application form.
- If you're moving, include your new contact information and when it goes into effect on the application form. (Remember, notification of awards may be many months after your submission.)

A JUDGE'S CONFESSION

The truth is, I've read some, well, many very bad scripts as a script competition judge. As I said in chapter 4, in my experience as a judge, often we are asked to read only the first ten pages of a script, which means that your script must be gripping from the first line.

I enjoy being a judge, and I love finding that winning script that has knocked my socks off. Unfortunately, more than my socks have been knocked off—I have been knocked off my chair in despair with some of the scripts I've read. Lying on the floor, befuddled and perplexed, I ramble: "Why did these entrants spend their hard-earned money on photocopying, postage, and entry fees with a script that is not industry-formatted, has typos, grammatical errors, pages missing, pages doubled, with coffee stains, and cat hair!"

Some of the scripts I've read had a great first ten pages, but then it's downhill from there. With other scripts I've read, I can't figure out where the story is going, what it's about, what the genre is, or who the main character is. Or there was nothing unique about the script that set it apart from the others.

I think the worst competition scripts I've read are the ones where underneath the scene heading the writer has synopsized what he or she intends to write for that scene in a later draft. I even read one script where the writer stated on the last page that he didn't know how he was going to end the story. Why did the writer submit a script before it was finished?! I've also read scripts where the writer has illustrations throughout the script. It's a *screenplay,* not a picture book!

Most judges are not paid a great deal of money to judge a competition. We do it because we want to give something back. We want writers to succeed, to win, and to get their movies made. We don't want to suffer from back injuries from falling off our chairs.

Judges have industry knowledge; they know what's been produced and what's in development. However, judges are not necessarily looking for scripts that have the potential to be good movies or commercial appeal. They're looking for the best script. Given this, high-concept scripts do not necessarily have a better chance of winning than a noncommercial script.

ON A SCALE OF ONE TO TEN . . .

Over the years I have judged many competitions, and like most judges I must read numerous scripts in a short period of time. I rate each script from one to ten. With each script, I write a couple of paragraphs of notes whether it's required of me or not. These notes include the merits of the script and the writer's talent and knowledge of the craft. After reading the script, I compare them to each other, decide on the finalists, and create my list.

There have been various scenarios as to how a competition winner is named. Here are two examples. Once my finalist list is completed, the competition coordinator will arrange a phone conference with the other judges and together we determine the winners. Or I will submit my list to the competition coordinator, and then a final judge (usually a famous industry name) will read all the other judges' finalist lists and from these select the winning screenplay.

In my experience, the judges have been in agreement about the top five or top ten finalists. The judges' feedback is sometimes subjective, but in the end we base our decisions on the most unique, well-crafted, and, of course, best script. The bottom line: Be passionate about your material and submit only your best work.

GRANTS, FELLOWSHIPS, AND ARTISTS COLONIES

It's important to seek every possible opportunity to get your work *noticed.* There are private and government grants and fellowships available for screenwriters. Listings can be found in film and screenwriting publications. *(See the appendix on page 257.)*

Receiving funding is a win-win situation. It's not only advantageous for your wallet, but it's also an impressive credit to add to your résumé.

Additionally, there are many artists' colonies throughout the country that provide screenwriters with a quiet place to work as well as the opportunity to network with other screenwriters and filmmakers.

TREATED LIKE A QUEEN

Over the years I have received fifteen grants and fellowships, which have certainly been an added financial bonus, but they have always led to more opportunities for my scripts to be read by those in the industry and opened more doors.

Artists' colonies have been a real slice of heaven, particularly the ones like the MacDowell Colony, at which I was fortunate to have been a fellow. Three wonderful meals are provided (lunch is delivered to your studio's doorstep in a picnic basket so you're not disturbed), bedding is changed, and the only concern you have each day is how many hours you write. Aside from this red-carpet treatment, the chance to live for a period of time with other writers, filmmakers, artists, and musicians is very inspiring and a good chance to network in a beautiful and relaxed environment. For me it offered an opportunity to collaborate on work with my fellow artists. As years go by, alumni parties and events give us a chance to reestablish old friendships and often discover new work opportunities.

CHAPTER TEN

FINDING AN AGENT. AND HALLELUJAH, I'VE GOT AN AGENT! NOW WHAT?

Finding an agent is tough and often exasperating work, and it may even feel like a full-time job for a while. You may encounter a lot of rejection, but be persistent and don't take it personally. Almost every writer has gone through the same hell. You must feel strongly about your screenplay, and that should be your inspiration to forge ahead.

Keep in mind that agents have a tremendous workload. They promote their clients at meetings, submit their clients' work, read their clients' scripts, and often give notes, attend clients' script readings, determine the appropriate company for their clients' scripts, set up pitch meetings for their clients, negotiate deals, seek additional talent by reading queries and scripts of prospective clients, and meet with those new potential prospects.

SAGE ADVICE

Here are some words of wisdom from my friend who's now hit the big time as a writer and executive producer:

"You shouldn't worry about getting an agent unless you're sure you have the next great script. Agents need heat to sell you, and really you get that for yourself when you write a great script. Also, it's better to find someone who really knows a great script when they see one.

"And how to convince a writer his or her script isn't ready? That's tough, but writers must get feedback from a good script consultant and/or an industry professional. Many of the bigger agents don't get you a job unless you've already had writing jobs or something produced. Hire a lawyer if you need a contract negotiated."

I realize that some of his advice sounds like a catch-22, but again the bottom line is that your great script is going to get you noticed!

FREQUENTLY ASKED QUESTIONS

How do I really get an agent?

There's no shortcut: you have to write a great script, query, and synopsis, and prepare a dazzling pitch. Without question, a personal recommendation from an industry professional gives you the edge over the competition, but whether or not you have industry contacts you must educate yourself about the business and you must network.

- **Attend script and film events.** If you do not live in Los Angeles or New York, where meeting agents may be easier because of proximity, you can attend reputable screenwriting conferences and film and pitch festivals where agents are speaking on panels. Try to meet them in person during the event. Agents who agree to speak on panels know that there are hungry writers out in the audience looking for representation, and often they are open to meeting new writers in order to find that new talent. If you do not get a chance to meet an agent at that event, then follow up with a letter stating that you attended the event and would like to have the opportunity to send him or her a synopsis of your project.

- **Read the trades.** *Variety* and *The Hollywood Reporter*, for example, list spec scripts written by new talent that have been optioned or bought by production companies and studios. Often they will list the agent who represented the script. Track these agents and contact them. You must immerse yourself in the business so you'll be well versed in who's who and the work they are doing. *(See the appendix on page 257 for more listings.)*
- **Watch movies.** Track the screenwriters you respect. Find out who represents them and then query those agents. *(See the appendix on page 257.)*
- **Network.** Even the most obscure contacts can lead to finding an agent.

MANY DEGREES OF SEPARATION

Years ago I went to a party hosted by film director Yvonne Rainer, who had been my film instructor at the Whitney Independent Study Program. There I met a nice older gentleman, a painter, who was wearing jeans and a T-shirt. He complimented me on one of my short films he had seen at a festival, and he happened to mention that his daughter-in-law was the head of development for a then-prominent production company and might be interested in seeing my work. With his urging, I contacted her. We hit it off; she read two of my spec scripts, and she called her good friend (who happened to be the head motion picture agent at a major agency). The agent and I met; he (or more likely one of his story analysts) read my scripts, and he recommended one of the agents from his department to represent me.

Do I pay an agent a reading fee?

Never. A WGA signatory agent is not permitted to charge a reading fee. An agent is permitted to take only ten % of the fee you receive for a writing assignment or script sale.

Is it worthwhile signing with a new agent at a respected agency?

Many screenwriters feel that new agents are hungrier and need to put their names on the map, so it is often to your benefit to have someone who needs to go that extra mile.

Is it important to have more than one script completed?

If you have several finished writing samples, this illustrates to the prospective agent that you are not a one-hit wonder. Having scripts in different genres may also be helpful in order to show your diversity as a writer.

If an agent sends a letter saying that he or she is not interested at this time in my script but that I should send other material, is this sincere?

Yes. This is a positive sign. Agents are busy and don't have time to waste. An agent may feel that the work you submitted illustrated your talent but was not something he or she could sell. Send another writing sample!

What are packaging agencies, and should I query them?

A packaging agency represents various talent, not only writers, but also above-the-line talent, including directors and actors. They will try to package your project in-house, which means that their goal is to get the team together with people they represent so that in the end they can receive a larger commission. If you have a commercial, mainstream project, then a packaging agency such as CAA, ICM, or William Morris might be the place to go.

Agents at the big packaging agencies seek screenwriters who write with an eye toward the market. High-concept scripts with big commercial potential, main characters that will attract A-list actors, and/or a story compelling enough to appeal to A-list directors increase the chances of the script getting optioned or sold.

Smaller or quirky stories are a tough sell and seldom grab agents' attention at packaging agencies unless, for example, the script has won or placed as a top finalist in a prestigious screenplay competition.

The advantage of being represented by or signing with a packaging agency is that they have direct access to above-the-line talent, which may increase your chances of getting your script made.

The downside of a packaging agency is that often they provide less personal support because their workload is heavier. They also may lose interest in you faster if your script(s) have not been getting any interest and/or if you're not getting writing assignments. In addition, since packaging agencies represent very experienced screenwriters, a studio may buy a film package knowing that the agency will get one of their own experienced screenwriters to rewrite your script. Or you may wait a long time until one of their signed directors or actors is available to do your project.

What does the term "hip-pocket" mean?

This term describes the relationship between an agent and a screenwriter in which an agent agrees to represent and submit material on behalf of a screenwriter without signing a contract with the screenwriter. Generally this occurs when an agent works for a big packaging agency and is not ready to commit a huge amount of time and the agency's money to promote the writer's work. It can be viewed as a trial period for the agent to see whether or not he or she can find interest in the writer's work and if the relationship with the writer is compatible.

The downside of being hip-pocketed is that the writer doesn't have the agent's full attention. The writer must do most of the legwork and establish contacts, network, and the rest of the groundwork in order to make things happen. In some cases, writers must submit their own scripts, but they can use the agency's name on the script's cover.

The upside is that when the writer makes contacts, stating that he or she has representation will help to spark someone's interest and, in turn, the agent will submit the script, do the follow-up, and negotiate the deal. If the writer succeeds in making contacts, continues to write and deliver good scripts, then this helps increase his or her chances of eventually getting signed with the agency.

Since there is no contract, the writer or agent can end

their relationship at any time. If you're unhappy with the agent or vice versa, then the relationship is over. Some writers have found success in a hip-pocket relationship, while others feel that their time and money has been wasted. Each agent-writer relationship is different, and there are always pros and cons to being hip-pocketed.

SHOOTING FROM THE HIP; OR, SHOOTING MYSELF IN THE FOOT

When I began my screenwriting career, I had two separate hip-pocket relationships with my agents. I didn't know enough about how the industry worked to realize that I had to continue developing contacts and get people interested in my work. I sat back and waited for my agents to make this happen. I didn't work with my agents to strategize a plan of action. I was also too shy to pick up the phone and remind my agents that I still existed. I didn't want to bother them. I thought they were actively working on my behalf. I was wrong.

With the first agent, the relationship was short-lived. With the second agent, I learned to be more assertive and make contacts, and I called my agent to check in, but it would take weeks before my call was returned.

In hindsight, I realized that I wasn't topping their priority lists because I needed to be more assertive from the onset in both relationships. I can't blame them for not having belief in me; I hadn't proved myself to them by showing that, not only was I a talented writer (they wouldn't have agreed to represent me otherwise), but that I had industry savvy and was ready and able to take on the business.

What is the difference between a boutique agency and a literary agency, and how do they differ from packaging agencies?

There is no difference; literary agencies are often referred to as "boutique agencies." Some literary agencies specialize in screenwriters, while others may also represent playwrights, television writers, fiction writers, and nonfiction writers. The downside of a literary agency is that it may take a long time to package an original script if the agency's access to talent (directors, producers, actors) is limited.

Similar to agents working in packaging agencies, the literary agent's job is to promote, sell, and/or option the screenwriter's work, negotiate contracts, seek out writing assignments, and oversee the marketing of subsidiary rights. Some literary agencies may have more time to work on building their clients' careers than agents in packaging agencies. Some literary agents work with their clients to polish their scripts and/or their pitches.

Literary agents may encourage you to sell or option your script to a producer with a studio deal, and the producer, in turn, will use the studio's resources to package the project. Although this is positive, it does increase the chances that you will lose control over your script.

What is client stealing; and should I, an aspiring screenwriter, worry?

No need to set your security alarms! Client stealing is when one agency lures a writer away from his or her current agency in order to represent them. This usually occurs when the writer is suddenly in demand and is beginning to reach a level of success. Generally, larger agencies are the *culprits* offering promises of lucrative deals and assignments to a writer who is currently represented by a smaller agency.

This puts the writer in a predicament. While the chance of more assignments and big money is certainly enticing, some writers choose to remain faithful to their current agents, who have devoted precious time building their careers. Some writers who do leave their current agencies feel it's worth the gamble and that it may carry more clout to say they're represented by a big agency. But the results are mixed; some writers have found success with the bigger agencies, while others are quickly lost in the agencies' large client roster and find no success.

WHAT AGENTS ACTUALLY DO

- Agents seek writing assignments for their clients and sell their spec scripts.
- Agents submit scripts to production companies, studios, and talent, and follow up to make sure that your work is getting read.
- Agents act on your behalf to set up pitch meetings and interviews with production companies and studios.
- Agents negotiate salary and contracts.
- Agents work with writers to plan career objectives and to map out strategies for meeting them.

HOW AN AGENT CAN WORK WITH YOU

Once your agent reads your script, he or she gives you story notes. Together you will then strategize the appropriate companies to submit your work to. Once you've compiled a list of prospective companies, your agent will contact a company's development executive and pitch your project. (Development executives read scripts and select those that are a right match for their company.)

Depending on your script's genre (for example, high-concept action), your agent will send a script out wide (to many companies), or (if your script is not high-concept) it will be sent to more discerning companies, such as a talent-based production company that is seeking scripts for particular talent or just to produce.

Your agent gives the development executive a brief time (sometimes one to two days) to decide on your project since other companies that your agent has submitted your script to are also making their decisions. Meanwhile, a producer who learned about your script through a tracking site and is interested in your project contacts your agent.

Everyone loves your script! Your agent's phone rings off the hook. Several offers from various companies are presented to your agent, who then must determine the best producer for your project. Now the roles are reversed: you've gone from selling yourself to your prospective agent to getting agent representation, to your agent pitching your project (in effect selling both of you to the development executive), to development executives selling themselves to your agent. Now you're in the starring role: your script is sold and your name is on the industry map!

WHAT TO DO WHEN MEETING A PROSPECTIVE AGENT

Your first meeting is like a first date. It's important to be punctual, dress appropriately, and be congenial. This may sound obvious, but as on a first date, each of you is assessing the other to see if this is indeed going to be a match.

- Don't be afraid of the agent. Show confidence but not overconfidence. An agent wants to know that you are articulate, can stand up for yourself, and will represent his or her agency well.
- Express what are reasonable and realistic expectations and ask what expectations the agent may have for you. For example, suggesting your script(s) be sent to five hundred companies per month and that you *expect* fifty pitch meetings weekly is not reasonable or realistic (or doable). Suggesting your script(s) be sent out to at least five or ten companies per month and that you hope to have at least two pitch meetings per month is a plausible request.
- At the end of your meeting, don't overstay your welcome.

YOUR AGENT SHOULD:

- have integrity, a good reputation, and connections in the film industry;
- understand your work and share your vision and sensibility;
- respond positively to your statement of your expectations.

You are establishing a working relationship with an agent, and it's important that you are comfortable with each other. Trust your instincts to determine if a given agent is the best person to champion your work. This is a business relationship not a friendship. Don't be afraid to ask questions.

QUESTIONS TO ASK A PROSPECTIVE AGENT

Whom do you represent?

Agents should be forthcoming regarding their client list. Certainly, it's most beneficial if the agent represents clients who are working steadily, as this is a positive reflection on the agent's ability and industry clout.

What type of contacts do you have with other companies and talent?

You want an agent who has established and extensive contacts in the industry in order to increase that agent's opportunities to sell your spec script and/or find you writing assignments.

How many writers does your agency represent, and how many do you represent?

If the ratio of writers to agents is high—more than fifty writers to one agent—question whether this is the right agent/agency for you.

Can I call you weekly or have regular strategy meetings?

Calling or e-mailing an agent once a week or biweekly and scheduling strategy meetings every few months is a legitimate request.

Will you read my new work? If so, how long should I wait to receive feedback?

You want an agent who will read your new work within approximately one month.

How do agents fit into the query-synopsis-pitch scenario?

You need to prepare a query, synopsis, and pitch whether or not you have an agent. If you do not have an agent, you should send queries to agents/agencies when seeking representation. If an agent is interested in your query, then he or she may request a synopsis of your script as well as the script. Then, if the agent likes your writing, he or she may ask you for a meeting, at which time you may be asked to pitch other story ideas to them. The pitch meeting will be an important part of their evaluation process because the agent will need to see how comfortable and professional you are with pitching.

If you do have an agent, get your agent's consent before sending queries out to production companies, studios, and talent. Your agent must know whom you are contacting in order to avoid overlaps, which would look unprofessional. (Some agents may want to be responsible for making all the contacts, so be sure that you and your agent are clear about this.) Once you have your agent's okay, state in your query that you have agent representation. This will certainly bring more attention to your letter.

Will you contact me prior to turning down an offer from a producer and/or production entity?

This is no secret: the higher the fee you receive for a writing assignment, the higher the agent's commission. Obviously, the agent wants to receive the highest commission possible. However, you may want to work on a project that is personally or artistically satisfying but not particularly high paying. It's important that an agent always consults with you when an offer is presented so you will have the option to decide whether or not you want to accept the assignment.

THE LAST TO KNOW

A producer and director whose work I respected asked me to send him a writing sample. They were looking for a new project to produce. I had my agent submit my script and then time passed. A lot of time. Finally, I called my agent to ask the status of the project. He proudly told me that an offer to option my script had been made—but that he had turned it down because it wasn't enough money. I was livid that he had not even contacted me. I frantically called the producer to try to salvage the project, but it was too late. They had chosen another script. Soon after, the producer-director team went on to make award-winning films, and I asked to be released from my contract with the agency. And my script was never produced.

HALLELUJAH, I'VE GOT AN AGENT!

Congratulations! Go out and celebrate! But if you think you can finally sit back and relax, don't get too comfortable. Remember, your agent alone doesn't get you work; you *and* your work get you work.

NOW WHAT?

- Keep your producer's cap on.
- You are essentially representing the agency every time you present your work, so be professional at pitch meetings.
- Agents will expect you to continue writing new and *great* scripts. Having several scripts in various genres will further help your agent to market you.
- Inform your agent of all your previous and current relationships with other producers, talent, and companies, and/or if any of your scripts has attachments. If any of these contacts are particularly solid, ask if it's more effective if you or your agent follow up with them.
- Provide your agent with a list of prior submissions to other producers, agents, companies, and/or talent and if they did coverage on any of your work. Even if the submissions were made years earlier, overlaps can backfire and make your agent look unprofessional.
- Let your agent know if you, as the writer, are attached to direct any of your scripts.
- Be accessible. Provide your agent with your current mailing address, phone numbers, and e-mail address. Keep your agent current so he or she knows where you can be reached should an unexpected meeting or assignment arise.
- If you are seeking a manager in addition to your present agent, discuss the pros and cons with your agent.
- If you have an attorney you want to use or need a recommendation for one, discuss this with your agent. Many agents are open to working with an attorney, but he or she must be an experienced entertainment attorney. Packaging agencies, for example, have their own in-house attorneys.

- Find out if your agent requires you to provide him or her with submission copies and if so, the number of copies needed.
- Keep the lines of communication open with your agent and continue to discuss your respective expectations about your relationship, including: (1) strategies to approach new contacts; (2) submission ideas; (3) if your agent intends to work with you to develop new ideas; (4) if your agent wants to be the sole person making contacts on your behalf; and (5) how often (weekly, biweekly, monthly) your agent wants you to check in with him or her.
- Discuss with your agent your respective requirements if: (1) your screenplay is optioned; (2) your screenplay is sold; and (3) you are offered a writing assignment.
- You must continue to network and make contacts in the industry. Telling these contacts that you have representation will spark their interest.
- If your agent gives you script notes, be open to feedback.
- Become your agent's agent. You must continue to develop hit lists of talent and companies that you are interested in approaching. Giving this list to your agent will not only illustrate your business savvy, but it also will cut down on your agent's workload, which will be appreciated.
- Be patient. Don't expect to have your spec script sold or get a writing assignment right away. If you're lucky, it may take a few months. Realistically, it takes about a year to get a new writer's work read and into the right hands. Try not to get discouraged.

CHAPTER ELEVEN

ENTERTAINMENT ATTORNEYS—A DIFFERENT KIND OF ADVOCATE

WHY YOU MAY NEED AN ENTERTAINMENT ATTORNEY

Here are some possible scenarios for hiring an entertainment attorney:

1. A company wants to option your script, but you don't have an agent to negotiate your contract. Since you need a contract that will protect your best interests, hiring an entertainment attorney will be a wise safeguard.
2. While waiting for a response from prospective agents, you can hire an entertainment attorney to represent you. Entertainment attorneys with strong connections to the film industry may submit scripts on behalf of their clients, and this may be an option for writers without agent representation. Many Hollywood studios and independent production companies are open to having scripts submitted by entertainment attorneys who are established in the film community.
3. You have agent representation, but you have questions about a pending contract. Although the

agency may have an in-house legal counsel, getting an outside opinion from your own entertainment attorney may provide objective insight and best serve your needs.

FREQUENTLY ASKED QUESTIONS

Can I forego seeking agent representation by hiring an entertainment attorney?

Yes, although having an agent may get you more attention if you're just starting out. There are many successful screenwriters who use entertainment attorneys instead of agents. Ultimately, companies are looking for a great script. An entertainment attorney with strong industry connections may be able to cover the same ground as an agent in terms of getting your script read.

Is it important to shop around, or should I just hire the first entertainment attorney who wants to work with me?

Definitely shop around. Don't rush into a relationship without being certain that the entertainment attorney has the right experience and connections and is the right person for you.

What can an entertainment attorney do that an agent cannot?

Entertainment attorneys and agents may both submit scripts on their clients' behalf, negotiate contracts, set up meetings, and so forth. However, entertainment attorneys may produce films whereas agents may not.

How do I find an entertainment attorney?

Trust your instincts and do research. *(See the appendix on page 257.)*

- **WORD OF MOUTH.** Ask your friends or colleagues for recommendations.

- **SEE FILMS.** The closing credits of a film usually list the entertainment attorney(s). If you admire the film and it seems like a good match with your script, contact the law firm.

- **READ THE TRADES.** Entertainment attorneys who have negotiated contracts for screenwriters are often listed in articles in the trades. If the script appears to be in the genre or style that you are working in, contact the law firm.

- **ATTEND SCREENWRITING CONFERENCES AND FILM FESTIVALS.** Entertainment attorneys often speak on panels, and this is a good opportunity to see and hear them in action.

WHAT TO LOOK FOR IN AN ENTERTAINMENT ATTORNEY

- Integrity, a good reputation, and film industry connections
- Initiative to get your work read in the industry
- Understanding of your work
- A positive response to your expectations

WHAT TO ASK AN ENTERTAINMENT ATTORNEY

Do you charge for the initial consultation meeting?

Usually this is free, but be sure to find out beforehand so you're not surprised with a bill.

Do you charge a percentage of the sale of my spec script, or do you charge on an hourly basis?

Being charged a percentage rather than an hourly fee may be preferable since you will not have to invest the money up front. However, attorneys want to be compensated for their time, and understandably they may not want to agree to this arrangement.

If you negotiate a writing assignment contract, will you charge a percentage of my writing fee or an hourly fee?

As stated above, a percentage may be preferable since you don't have to put out the money without a sale or writing assignment. However, if the contract is considered a straightforward standard contract, then it may be to your benefit to pay the hourly fee, which may be less than the lawyer's percentage.

What contacts do you have with agents, studios, production companies, producers, and talent?

You want an attorney who has established film-industry relationships so your work will be seriously considered.

How many screenwriters do you and the law firm represent?

You want an attorney and/or law firm that has a successful track record representing screenwriters.

Will you assist me in getting my career launched? If so, what is your strategy?

Some attorneys will only submit scripts on the writer's behalf, while others will also provide career strategies, give packaging assistance, target companies, and provide general follow through.

Will you initiate the contacts with studios, production companies, producers, and talent on my behalf, or do you expect me to do this?

If you don't have any contacts, certainly, it's best if an attorney can initiate them, but don't be dissuaded from hiring an attorney who will not initiate contacts. Remember, you need to always wear your producer's cap and provide hit lists to attorneys.

Can I call you biweekly or have regular strategy meetings?

Unlike agents, attorneys will usually charge an hourly fee for consultations.

Will you read my new work, and if so, how long should I expect to wait to receive feedback?

You want an attorney who reads your new work within approximately one month and, at the very least, gives you general feedback as to whether he or she feels the script is ready for submission and which companies and/or talent to target.

Will you contact me prior to turning down an offer?

This is *your* career; you do not want to be the last to know of a missed opportunity that might have best served you.

CHAPTER TWELVE

THEY LIKE ME! THEY REALLY LIKE ME! (OR AT LEAST THEY SAY THEY DO)

THE OPTION AGREEMENT AND DEVELOPMENT DEAL

They like you! They really like you! And why do they like you? You've rewritten your spec script to perfection. You've written an attention-getting query and a stunning synopsis. You've delivered the perfect pitch. You've persevered. You didn't give up no matter how many rejections you received. You've networked your little heart out, and you've spoken to and met with anyone and everyone connected to the film industry no matter how remote the connection seemed to be. Now, if luck continues to stay on your side, one of two things may happen: *They'll* want to buy *your* script. (Your script will be optioned.) Or, *they'll* want to hire *you* to write a script for them. (You enter into a development deal.)

This is the moment you've been striving for. You're there! You've arrived! Now what?

THE OPTION AGREEMENT

What is an option agreement?

If a company is interested in producing your spec script, its first step will usually be an offer to option your script. An option agreement means that the producer or production entity is buying the exclusive rights to purchase your script within a specified period of time and for a specified price.

How much can I get paid for an option fee?

There is no standard option fee; fees are negotiable. It can be a token fee of one dollar or a more substantial fee of $1,000 to $10,000 or more. The amount depends on the type of script (high-concept/mainstream or art house) and the producer or production entity's economic backing (independent production company or studio). Often the option fee is 10 percent of the purchase price.

For example, if your script is optioned for $5,000, then the purchase price of your script will be $50,000.

If at the end of the option period (which can be anywhere from six to eighteen months, depending on the deal) the producer has raised the financing to produce your script, and exercises the option, you will receive the balance of $45,000. Or, if the option period ends and no financing has been secured, you keep the initial option fee of $5,000, and you may enter into a new deal with a new producer or production entity.

What is a "purchase price," and how much can I expect it to be?

The purchase price is the fee that you will receive for your spec script. Like option fees, purchase prices are negotiable.

Generally, the purchase price is between 2 percent and 5 percent of the film's budget.

If you are a member of the WGA or if the producer is signatory to the WGA, then the WGA Basic Agreement for union-mandated minimums applies. The WGA Schedule of Minimums can be found on their Web site at www.wga.org. If you are not a WGA member, try to negotiate a purchase price comparable to the one WGA members receive.

What happens during the option period?

During the option period the producer or production entity will try to secure financing, attach talent to the film, and possibly arrange domestic and foreign presales. Additionally, you may be asked to do rewrites, which you may or not be paid for depending on your contract.

Since the producer/production entity now has the exclusive rights to your spec script, you may not have this script optioned by another producer during the option period.

What is an option extension?

In your option agreement there may be a renewal or extension clause, which means that you agree to the producer's right to renew his or her option for a specified amount of time for an additional payment should the producer need more time to secure financing. Usually the option extension payment is not applied against the purchase price, which means that it is not deducted from the payment you will receive from the sale of your spec script.

What does the term "exercising the option" mean?

This means the producer/production entity that has optioned your spec script is now going to buy it. The ownership rights of your spec script will be transferred from you, the writer, to the producer/production entity, and you will be paid the purchase price. Once the option is exercised, you can no longer option or sell this script to anyone else.

YOUR OPTION AGREEMENT CONTRACT

Under no circumstances should you negotiate your own contract. If you don't have an agent, hire an experienced entertainment attorney to negotiate your contract. It is definitely worth the investment.

WHAT TO ASK FOR

- **CREDIT:** Be sure that you are properly credited for your work. If you are a WGA member or the producer/production entity is a WGA signatory, the WGA will determine your credit. Generally, the credit will be the same size on the screen as the director's and will appear before the director's credit in the main titles of the film. Additionally, credits should appear in all advertising and on the DVD and/or video box. If this is not a WGA agreement, then your credit will be negotiated. It is in your best interest to model your contract to the standard WGA guidelines as cited above.

- **EXCLUSIVITY:** Your goal is to be the sole screenwriter of the film. Getting exclusivity may be difficult unless you are an established writer, but it's worth negotiating.

- **REWRITES:** There are two main points to consider when negotiating your rewrite fee: (1) Be sure that the expected number of rewrites is clearly stated in your contract, otherwise you may be doing endless rewrites without compensation; (2) your rewrite fees should be separate from the purchase price, otherwise you will earn less money.

- **PERCENTAGE OF PROFITS:** It is reasonable for a writer to seek a percentage of the profits. Generally, asking for 2 to 5 percent of the net is acceptable. However, it's unlikely that you will ever see any percentage of the profits due to the unfortunate fact that production companies and studios often hide the true profits behind false production expenses—often referred to as "creative accounting."

- **SEQUELS:** You may want to negotiate to write any sequels to your original script. You may ask for the "first right of refusal," which means that you will be the first writer to be offered the job of writing the sequel, but you will have the right to turn it down. Additionally, you may negotiate a fee or percentage of the profits from any sequels if you are not the writer.

- **SPIN-OFFS, SERIES EPISODES, AND REMAKES:** You may negotiate a fee or a percentage for each of these three items.

- **ANCILLARY RIGHTS:** If the film becomes a hit like *Shrek* or *Toy Story* (usually this applies to kids' films or animated films), then lunch boxes, records, toys, books, and such will be manufactured. It's important to negotiate a percentage of the profits from sales of these items.

THE DEVELOPMENT DEAL

What is a development deal and how do I get one?

Generally, a producer or production entity, after reading your spec script (as a writing sample) or hearing your outstanding pitch, will offer you a development deal. They will pay you a fee to write a screenplay for them, which they own all rights to.

What does this mean for me?

You are essentially a hired gun, an employee of the producer. It is your job to translate the ideas of the person hiring you onto the page and into a great script. This may be quite a challenge. Ultimately, it is the person hiring you who will make the final script decisions, so remember to be diplomatic when you suggest ideas or try to make changes.

What will the deal comprise of?

Writers are usually presented with a step deal. You will be paid in stages against the total purchase price of your script. These stages may include: (1) an advance payment before you begin work; (2) payment for your treatment; (3) payment for a first draft; (4) payment for a second draft; and (5) final payment for a polish. (Often, a writer can negotiate a bonus payment if the film is produced.)

The downside of this deal is that at any time during this process you can be eliminated from the project.

Is there really a Development Hell?

Yes, Virginia, there really is a Development Hell, and it is comprised of endless rewrites and changes and tweaks to the script you have been hired to write. What they loved yesterday, they hate today. Or a producer's mother just read the new draft and didn't like the main female teen character and thinks this character should be changed to a gay, male, senior citizen. You get the picture.

RELAX, IT'S ONLY A MOVIE

INT. SUSAN'S MANHATTAN APARTMENT - MIDDLE OF THE NIGHT

A Little Italy railroad flat. Posters cover the crumbling walls. Papers are strewn across the floor.

Susan paces in front of her desk. Dressed in striped black-and-white pajamas, which resemble a prison jumpsuit, many pencils poke through her hair.

Susan stops pacing, pours the last drops of old coffee from the coffeepot into her mug. She reads the text on her mug.

SUSAN

"Relax, it's only a movie!" Ha!

Susan quickly downs the thick liquid.

She SLAMS the mug on her desk and sits at her computer.

SUSAN (CONT'D)

Inferno! Abyss! Hades! This is my hell! How can I relax?!

The phone RINGS. Susan picks up, but before she can even say hello she hears:

PRODUCER #1 (ON PHONE)

Susan! I've got it! It's brilliant! It's--

SUSAN

It's one in the morning.

PRODUCER #1 (ON PHONE)

Not in L.A.--listen--the main character should be a flight attendant instead of a doctor. And she doesn't poison her sister; she saves her from a burning building. And I have a new name for her. Ready? Mitzi!

SUSAN

Mitzi?

PRODUCER #1 (ON PHONE)

I knew you'd love it. My daughter, the six year old, came up with it. Listen, my masseur is waiting for me. I am SO in knots tonight. Ta-ta.

Susan hangs up. Stares at her computer screen.

SUSAN

I know I should be grateful for having a writing job so I can finally pay my rent on time but--

The phone RINGS. Susan SIGHS, picks up the phone. What next?

SUSAN (CONT'D)

Hello?

PRODUCER #2 (ON PHONE)

I hope I'm not calling too late, but you know the trouble we've been having with Maya?

SUSAN

Who?

PRODUCER #2 (ON PHONE)

The main character.

SUSAN

First she's Tracy, the animal trainer; then she's Mitzi the--

PRODUCER #2 (ON PHONE)

Mitzi? Don't you think she should be called Ayla?

SUSAN

Who-la?

PRODUCER #2 (ON PHONE)

Sleep on it. You sound tired. Ciao.

Susan hangs up.

SUSAN

These producers *can't* even agree on the name of the main character let alone whether she is going to elope with her boyfriend or kill him?!

Exasperated, Susan BANGS her head against the computer monitor. Her coffee mug CRASHES to the floor.

Susan bends down and carefully picks up and examines a piece of the now chipped text from her broken mug. She shakes her head and reads aloud:

SUSAN (CONT'D)

"Relax."

Susan LAUGHS. She leans back in her chair, puts her feet on the desk. Takes a deep relaxing breath--and falls backward to the floor.

CHAPTER THIRTEEN

TIPS ON APPROACHING WRITING ASSIGNMENTS AND FINDING HARMONIOUS COLLABORATION

LIFE AS A WRITER-FOR-HIRE

Whether you've been hired to write or rewrite a script, you must understand the director and/or producer's goals for the project:

- Ask what initially inspired the story (was it a news story? a person? a dream?) and thoroughly research all aspects of the material, such as setting and time period.
- If this is a writing assignment, ask specific questions, such as: (1) What is the story that you want to tell? (2) Who do you see as the main characters, and what are the major obstacles they must overcome? (3) What is the genre?
- If this is a rewriting assignment, come to an agreement as to what *exactly* needs to be done. For example: (1) Do the characters need to be fleshed out? (2) Does the story structure need to be reworked or tightened? (3) Does the dialogue need fine-tuning?

- After these questions are agreed upon, submit an outline or a two-to-three-page treatment to confirm that you're all literally on the same page. This will help to avoid future problems.
- Keep the dialogue ongoing and honest with the people who hired you so there will be no surprises on either end.

BETTER THAN SEX

One rewrite assignment I was hired to do required working with the original screenwriter—I'll call him Bob. It was a very sensitive situation. Although Bob was a very talented writer, the producer who hired me felt that they had reached an impasse with the script. The script was essentially Bob's baby, and I was very aware of my delicate position on the project.

I approached working with Bob the same way I approached my role as the Su-City Pictures East screenplay doctor, and that was to be the objective eye on the project and to inject new and fresh ideas. Bob had lived with the script for several years and knew it backward and forward, while I had the advantage of seeing things from a new perspective. As time passed, Bob didn't act threatened by my presence on the project, and he even expressed relief to have me working with him.

On the night we completed the script, we were both ecstatic. The story and character problems were solved, and the script was finally working. It was time for Bob to type the final words: "The End." Bob took a deep breath and typed those final two words. Then he leaned back in his seat, exhaled, turned to me, and said, "This is better than sex."

KEYS TO BENDING WITHOUT BREAKING

Coauthoring and collaborating doesn't always match my experience with Bob. It also can be very exasperating if you are not in sync with your writing partner or with the person who hired you.

Put Your Cards on the Table

Doing this from the onset of the collaboration avoids hurt egos and surprises later on.

1. Clearly express your expectations and goals for the script and your collaboration, and ask what the other person has in mind.
2. Explain your writing process and work habits, and ask what your collaborator's process and work habits are. (For example: Are you a night or a day person? Do you want to write each scene together, work separately on different scenes, or work on drafts independently?)

Keep Your Goals in Mind

You want a great script. This sounds obvious, but when tensions run high (almost inevitable at some point in the collaborative process), keep your eye on the prize—the great, finished script.

Be Willing to Compromise Your Ideas and Listen to Your Partner

Compromising does not mean that you're selling out; it means that you are open to new ideas. You may discover that your partner has great ideas and inspiring suggestions that you never even considered or initially thought were terrible. Keep the lines of communication open to avoid any conflicts during this process.

CHAPTER FOURTEEN

YOUR SCREENWRITING MANTRAS

Congratulations! You are now on your way to becoming a savvy screenwriter, ready to enter the film industry. Here are the three final tips to ensure that your journey into this new world is a safe one. Repeat these—make them your mantras:

Preserve.

Never offer to work for free.

Always get a contract!

PERSEVERE

You have a great screenplay, but you keep hitting brick walls. Don't let this stop you. The competition is extremely tough, but if you believe in your project and are passionate, then you must not give up.

The film industry demands the survival of the most persistent—not necessarily the fittest. This may sound cynical, but often it's the truth. There are writers and filmmakers who may not be that talented but position themselves to get the big break. Yes, this is disheartening, but try to turn it around and use it as a powerful incentive to continue to knock on more doors, send out more queries, and drag yourself to yet one more networking event.

NEVER OFFER TO WORK FOR FREE

Maybe a director tells you he's going to produce your script for nothing or a fledgling production company tells you that you're going to get your first big break in exchange for your script. Proceed with caution!

This can be a wonderful chance to get your movie made, and the people interested in your script may be offering an incredible opportunity. But don't *you* make the offer to work for free. Ask *them* what they are planning to offer *you* first.

Offering to work for free might be a guaranteed ticket to disaster. There's a good chance you will be taken advantage of. Know your worth. A company should hire you because you are good, not because you are an easy target.

If a producer is very determined to get a film made and hires you because of your talent, then that producer must find a way to pay you a writing fee, even if it's just a small token fee. It's not your responsibility to worry about how they will come up with the money. Don't let the producer attempt to instill guilt. Raising money is the producer's job. Your job, and it *is* a job, is to get compensated for your work.

Do your research before you enter into any agreement with a producer and/or director. Find out the work they've produced in the past and the contacts they have with other companies and talent. (*See the appendix on page* 257.)

Don't be afraid to ask questions! If they're not forthcoming with answers, then ask yourself if this is the right deal for you. Always get a contract and have it reviewed by an entertainment attorney.

LESSONS LEARNED

I was overcome with joy when I was hired by an independent producer to adapt a novel for a screenplay. This was my first assignment. I was given a contract that the producer drew up. I did not have an entertainment attorney review it. (My first mistake.) The contract stated that I would receive payment upon first monies received from investors. I knew no investors were lined up yet, but I was willing to take the chance. (My second mistake.) I loved the novel and was so excited by this opportunity that I accepted the job. (My third mistake.)

I wanted to be seen as someone who was diligent and eager to work. And work I did. I did countless rewrites without compensation. (My fourth mistake.) The number of rewrites I would be required to do was not included in the contract. (My fifth mistake connected to my first mistake—the one about not hiring an entertainment attorney.) But because I wanted to make a good impression and be part of the team, I thought this was okay. But it wasn't okay. Soon the producer saw me as one of those expendable writers, and I was pushed off the job. It was a tough lesson to learn.

ALWAYS GET A CONTRACT!

A handshake is only a handshake. If a producer, a production company, and/or the talent loves your work but doesn't want to ruin the friendship with legalities, think again—or better still, run. A contract will keep the friendship intact and protect your best interests.

Friends and Adversaries

EXT. NEW YORK CITY'S EAST VILLAGE - NIGHT

A bustling street filled with shops, restaurants, and STREET VENDORS. Susan, dressed in black, and DIRECTOR (50, ex-hippie who still looks, dresses, and acts the part) walk quickly as they seek out an inexpensive restaurant.

SUSAN

I have the contract with me. We can talk about it over dinner.

DIRECTOR

Contract?

SUSAN

The contract that we discussed last week. I had my lawyer draw it up. He was nice enough to barter with me. I did a critique of his script, and he drew up the contract in exchange.

DIRECTOR

That's cool. But, Susan, a contract? Contracts aren't my bag. I didn't agree to that.

SUSAN

Actually you did when we met last week. (takes a deep breath) I'm more comfortable working with a contract.

DIRECTOR

Contracts make friends into adversaries.

SUSAN

I've found that contracts keep friends--friends.

DIRECTOR

You know I'm good for the dough.

SUSAN

(warning bells go off)

I haven't seen any dough yet and I've worked with you for three months now and--

DIRECTOR

(interrupts, points to restaurant)

I really dig Indian food. How 'bout it?

SUSAN

(frustrated)

Actually, it doesn't agree with me.

INT. SUSAN'S LIVING ROOM - THAT NIGHT

Susan lies on her futon, one hand clutches her stomach; the other holds a pile of bills.

Kate (green hair and matching green outfit) comes in from the kitchen with a cup of tea and gives it to Susan.

SUSAN

Thanks for coming over and taking care of me. (sips tea) Why didn't I just stamp "sucker" on my forehead?

KATE

How did you know that creep of a director had no intention of paying you?

SUSAN

I've been working in this business long enough to have known better. (looks at bills) Now, I'm going to have to go back to reading six scripts

```
     a night for the studios to come up with this
     month's rent.

Kate flops down on a nearby chair.

                         KATE
     This is so depressing. Tell me something
     positive will come from all of this.

Susan holds up her hand as if taking an oath.

                         SUSAN
     I swear I will never work without a contract
     again, and never, I mean never, eat Indian food
     again.

                         KATE
     Touché.

They CLINK teacups.
```

A contract is only good if both parties sign it. If you don't have an agent, then hire an entertainment attorney to draw a contract up for you. If you can't afford an entertainment attorney, there are organizations like Volunteer Lawyers for the Arts that can assist you. (*See the appendix on page* 257.)

Never sign a contract without an attorney reviewing it first. A good contract will enable you to get recourse should a problem arise!

So Sue Me

INT. VOLUNTEER LAWYERS FOR THE ARTS OFFICE - DAY

A modest Manhattan office. Susan, dressed in another black outfit, is seated across from VLA staff attorney JANE, 35, down-to-earth, tough.

Jane speaks on the phone as she reviews Susan's file.

JANE

Yes, in a nutshell, the producer broke Susan's contract by not paying the balance of her writing fee by the contractual deadline, which was first day of principal photography. (beat) Yes. Thanks very much.

Jane hangs up.

Susan nervously fidgets with her hair.

SUSAN

Do you think you can help me?

JANE

Yes. You meet our criteria.

SUSAN

It's reassuring to know that my income was low enough to be eligible for VLA's services.

JANE

(smiles)

Well, I believe your financial status is about to change. The A.B. law firm has agreed to represent you pro bono.

SUSAN

Wow! The A.B. law firm, otherwise known as the Amazingly Big law firm! They're one of the most powerful entertainment law firms in New York.

JANE

That's right, and they're as furious as I am that your contact was not honored. With A.B.'s involvement, it just may shake up this producer and even, dare I say--change his ways!

SUSAN

I like how you think!

Susan rises from her seat and shakes Jane's hand.

INT. SUSAN'S KITCHEN - TWO DAYS LATER

In the center of the kitchen is an old-fashioned clawfoot bathtub in which Susan, submerged underneath the bath bubbles, relaxes. Only her painted toenails are visible.

The phone RINGS on a nearby table. Susan ignores it. It RINGS twice more. Curiosity gets the better of her. She emerges from the bubbles, leans over and picks up the receiver.

SUSAN

Hello?

The bathwater SLOSHES.

PRODUCER (ON PHONE)

Susan, is that you? Are you underwater?

SUSAN

Yes, it's me--

PRODUCER (ON PHONE)

(angry)

I can't believe you did this!

SUSAN

(innocently)

Did what?

PRODUCER (ON PHONE)

How could you sue me?

SUSAN

(smiles)

How could you not pay me?

PRODUCER (ON PHONE)

But how could you sue me?

SUSAN

(enjoys the moment)

But how could you not pay me?

PRODUCER (ON PHONE)

Susan! How could you sue me?!

SUSAN

(*really* enjoys this)

Thanks for the check. It arrived today.

PRODUCER (ON PHONE)

How did you afford to get the Amazingly Big law firm to represent you?

SUSAN

That was your first mistake. You underestimated me. Never underestimate a screenwriter.

Susan hangs up the phone, smiles, and submerges herself in the bubbles.

EPILOGUE

What excites me the most about screenwriting is the opportunity to bring the stories, themes, and images in my head to life by translating them onto the screen. Having scripts produced has fulfilled my wish: challenging audiences to think and react, and perhaps even making a difference in their lives.

FAMILY TIES

It all started when I was a child. When my parents took me to the movies, I would insist on staying in the theater to see the film over and over . . . and yes, over again. It seemed perfectly normal to me. Then they took me to see the European and experimental films at the Museum of Modern Art in New York. These films were different from the ones in our local theater. They had overlapping narratives, poetic language, amazing color, and astounding images. I was awestruck. (I never could have imagined that many years later my own short films would be acquired for MoMA's permanent collection and archives.)

When I was a young teenager, my parents and I saw Louis Malle's film *Lacombe Lucien.* Set in World War II, the story centers on a Jewish family in hiding. The film was profoundly meaningful to our family because one of its stars was Therese Giehse—my great-great-aunt. Like other members of my family, Giehse narrowly escaped the Holocaust. (Giehse was a highly regarded German theater actress—her face even decorated a German postage stamp several years ago.)

Before seeing *Lacombe Lucien,* I had no aspirations to be a writer or filmmaker, but I was so inspired and moved, I knew that writing and filmmaking was somehow going to be a part of my life. I also knew that I wanted to meet Louis Malle.

In 1985 I found my opportunity. Malle was speaking at the screening of his documentary *God's Country* at the Carnegie Hall Cinema in Manhattan. After the event, he was swarmed with fans. I nervously waited until the crowd dwindled, and then I took my courage in hand and introduced myself: "I'm the great-great-niece of Therese Giehse, and I always wanted to meet you to tell you how much your film meant to me." Malle graciously shook my hand. I then dashed away. Suddenly, someone grabbed my shoulders. It was Malle. He asked me to repeat what I just told him. I did. He then hugged me and said: "I didn't know Giehse had any surviving relatives. Are you an actress?" I was so shy that I could only shake my head no.

Malle started pounding me with excited questions: "Where do you live? What do you do?" I managed to answer, but barely. Soon we developed a friendship, which led to the opportunity to work on his documentary *And the*

Pursuit of Happiness in 1986. I will never forget when he called me and asked, "Susan, would you like to work with me on my new film?" He didn't say, "work *for* me," and I was very struck by this. And indeed, the work environment he created was a team effort. I got hands-on experience doing research, production coordinating, interviewing, and working with Louis on story editing the voice-over narration. Louis was very generous and patient teaching me the ropes. His patience was only tested with me in one area, and that was my poor sense of direction. Inevitably, I would get lost no matter where I drove with him.

Having a personal connection certainly was an in to the film business, and I consider working with Louis my first big break. For better or worse the old adage "It's all about who you know" did apply, but only to a certain degree. Had I not had the experience making my six short films and working at several film companies, including Paramount Pictures, it's very unlikely that Louis would have hired me based purely on my family lineage. I still had to prove to myself and to Louis that I could do a good job. Wisely, Louis took no chances. He initially hired me for a two-week trial period—and I passed the test! I worked on the film from preproduction through postproduction. It was an experience I will always cherish.

After twenty-five years of working in the film industry, I still believe in the power of movies. Movies can influence and provoke, and become part of the cultural language. Movies change the way we see the world. It is a profound responsibility to communicate ideas to an audience. We screenwriters *can* make a difference. You can make a difference. Good luck!

Always Leave Them Laughing

INT. MANHATTAN BOOKSTORE - NIGHT

An easel with a poster of *The Savvy Screenwriter* is on display.

The EXCITED CROWD snatches up copies of *The Savvy Screenwriter*. Books fly off the shelves.

CROWD

This is just what I always needed! Hey, this is really funny. This is exactly what I was looking for. Can you believe all this great information she covers! I didn't think she could top her original book, but this new edition is even better.

LATER

The seated crowd holds copies of *The Savvy Screenwriter*.

Susan, now older (but won't reveal her age), with long reddish curly hair, and a colorful dress, stands at the podium.

SUSAN

Thank you all for coming tonight, and enjoy the book!

The audience leaps to their feet. A standing OVATION. A couple of screenwriters approach Susan.

SCREENWRITER #1

That was a great reading.

SUSAN

Thank you.

SCREENWRITER #2

(points at Susan)

Look! You really do have naturally curly hair!

SUSAN

Yes I do.

Susan smiles and tries not to laugh. There's always one in every audience!

Kate slides up next to Susan. She has shoulder-length, naturally blonde hair, and wears a conservative beige business suit.

KATE

You'll never guess who I saw on late night TV yesterday. Your *favorite* movie starlet.

SUSAN

Someone actually hired her after receiving the Atrocious Acting award for worst screen actress of the decade? What's the movie?

KATE

It's an *infomercial* about making your own 60s clothing. Gauze shirts, love beads--and guess who directed it?

SUSAN

Not the "so sue me" guy!

KATE

Indeed. I guess they're eating their just desserts.

SUSAN

Or eating crow!

KATE

Let's go celebrate--dinner's on me!

SUSAN

Great! You pick the restaurant--anything but Indian.

Susan and Kate LAUGH.

SUSAN (V.O.) (CONT'D)

Despite my independent roots, I couldn't resist the perfect--and predictable Hollywood ending.

FADE OUT

APPENDIX

SAVVY LINGO—GLOSSARY OF SCREENPLAY AND FILM TERMS

ABOVE-THE-LINE: A term describing budget fees for story, screenplay, producer(s), director, and cast.

ADAPTATION: A screenplay based on another source such as a novel, short story, magazine, or newspaper article.

AGENT: A person who represents clients and negotiates contracts on their behalf.

A-LIST: Talent/star whose name can potentially draw big box office and/or get a project made just by having his or her name attached.

AMBIANCE: A term describing the mood or feeling of a setting or scene.

ANGLE: A term describing the point of view from which the action is observed.

ANTAGONIST: An adversary whose objective is to prevent the protagonist from reaching his or her goal.

ARBITRATION: The Writers Guild of America's process to determine a disputed screenplay credit.

ASSOCIATE PRODUCER: A free-for-all! The definition of this credit varies, depending on the individual's role on the film. It can be given to the person working under the producer who shares in the creative and business duties, to a financier, or even to a person who brought the script or property to the producer.

ATTACHMENTS: Actors, director, and/or producers who agree to work on a film. These name attachments will often help to get a film financed and/or produced.

BACK END: The percentage of a film's profits contractually paid to name talent after the film is released.

BACKSTORY: A term used to describe the events in a character's life prior to the present events in the screenplay.

BEAT: A single dramatic moment or a single dramatic event in a screenplay.

BEAT SHEET: The breakdown of the scenes in a screenplay. Generally, the key scenes are the only ones included in a beat sheet.

BELOW-THE-LINE: A term referring to those budget costs for production and postproduction, including technicians, materials, and labor.

bg: The abbreviation for the word "background." In screenplays this refers to action, characters, or a general area that is seen behind the main action.

BIDDING WAR: A situation in which two or more buyers (such as studios or producers) make a bid on the same project.

B-LIST: Talent and/or stars who are considered second tier in terms of drawing big box office.

BOFFO: A slang word, often used in the Hollywood trades, meaning huge box-office receipts.

BOMB: The opposite of "boffo," meaning poor box-office receipts.

BUDGET: The financial breakdown of specific expenditures to produce a film.

BUZZ: What everyone in the film business is talking about—a hot project or talent considered to have enormous box-office potential.

CASTING DIRECTOR: The person or company who auditions, negotiates contracts, and hires the actors for a film. A casting director reports to the director and/or producer of the film.

CHARACTER ARC: The terminology most commonly used to describe a character's development from the beginning to the end of the script.

COPRODUCER: The definition of this credit varies, depending on the individual's role on the film. He or she can be sharing in the creative and business duties, or a financier, or even a person who brought the script or property to the producer.

CREATIVE ELEMENTS: Term used to describe the writer, actor(s), and/or director who have agreed to work on (become attached) a film project.

DEAL BREAKER: Term(s) of a contract negotiation that cannot be agreed upon, which can result in ending the negotiations.

DEAL MEMO: A fully and legally binding written agreement stating the terms of the forthcoming legal contract.

DEUS EX MACHINA: A term used to describe the resolution or end to a plot problem, which seems contrived, forced, or too implausible.

DEVELOPMENT: The process of developing a script or idea with the goal being a script ready for production.

DEVELOPMENT DEAL: An agreement in which a writer is hired by a production company or studio to work on the script, starting from either the idea stage or the first-draft stage and proceeding through several rewrites.

DEVELOPMENT HELL: What you want to avoid! The unenviable situation of being hired to develop a screenplay and having to write endless revisions often without proper compensation.

DIRECT-TO-VIDEO: A feature film that does not get released theatrically and is only released on home video.

DIRECTOR OF DEVELOPMENT or DEVELOPMENT EXECUTIVE: The person who oversees the development of a script and finds new material for the company to produce.

DISSOLVE TO: A screenplay or film term describing a visual change when one image fades out and another image fades in. Generally used to show a transition in time.

DISTRIBUTOR: The studio or distribution company that books the theaters for the film's release and supplies the prints.

DRAFT: A version of a screenplay that will later be rewritten.

ELEMENTS: Talent (actors, directors, known entities) who agree to work on the film.

END CREDITS: The cast and crew credits that are seen at the end of the film. Contracts will include specifications of the size of the credit and placement on the screen.

ESTABLISHING SHOT: In screenplay formatting, a term used to identify the location of a scene in the scene heading (slug line).

EXCLUSIVE DEAL: A term describing the housekeeping arrangement an actor, producer, or director's production company has with a producer (such as a studio).

EXECUTIVE PRODUCER: The credit given to the person who either finances or secures the financing for a film.

EXPLOITATION FILM: A film that contains gratuitous sex and violence.

EXPOSITION: Backstory or facts about the story or character.

EXT.: The abbreviation of the word "exterior," used in scene headings to indicate that the scene is taking place outside.

FADE-IN: Terminology used to describe an image that slowly appears from black. Although generally used to indicate the script's beginning, it is sometimes used to show time changes between scenes.

FADE-OUT: Terminology used to describe an image that slowly disappears until only black is seen on the screen. Generally used to indicate the script's end, it is sometimes used to show time between scenes or points in the story.

FEATURE: A film whose length is approximately two hours.

FILM NOIR: A genre wherein the story and characters are regarded as dark and mysterious. Generally, this genre includes a femme fatale, a crime, and betrayal. *Double Indemnity* is an example of a classic film noir.

FINANCIER: An individual or studio that invests their money to produce a film.

FIRST-LOOK DEAL: A term describing a company's right to see a writer or producer's project before it is submitted to other companies for consideration.

FLASHBACKS: Scenes that jump back in time to illustrate the history of a character or story. Flashbacks should be used with caution.

GREEN LIGHT: Green means Go! A term describing a script that has been approved for production.

GROSS: The total box-office earnings that a film has generated. This may also include video/DVD rentals and licensing fees.

HARD SELL: A script or idea that is considered noncommercial and/or difficult to sell.

HIGH-CONCEPT: A script or story idea that is considered extremely commercial. Also may be defined as a story idea that can be conveyed in one powerful sentence.

HOOK: A term used to describe a specific event (like the inciting incident) or a visual that grabs the executive's and/or audience's interest.

HOUSEKEEPING DEAL: An arrangement between an independent production company and a producer (such as a studio) whereby the producer, in exchange for funding the company's overhead, is given the sole right to see and then accept or reject any material the production company acquires.

IN THE CAN: A term used to describe a filmed scene or a film that has completed principal photography.

INCITING INCIDENT: A term used to describe the specific event occurring in Act 1 that advances the main plotline forward.

INDEPENDENT PRODUCER: A producer who develops material and finds financing for a project without being under contract with a studio.

INDEPENDENT PRODUCTION: A film that is not studio-financed. However, a studio may distribute a film that was independently produced.

INDIE: A term that describes both an independent film (a film not produced by a studio) and an independent production company (a company that works outside the studio system).

INT.: The abbreviation of the word "interior," used in scene headings to indicate that the scene is taking place inside.

LIMITED RELEASE: (1) A completed film (such as an art or a foreign film) that is marketed and screened to a targeted audience because of its specialized appeal; (2) a completed film that is first shown to small audiences to test-market their interest and may later be distributed in wider release to more theaters.

LINE PRODUCER: The person who supervises above-the-line and below-the-line elements during production.

LOGLINE: A one-sentence synopsis of a script.

LOOP: The process of rerecording or adding new dialogue or new sounds in postproduction.

LOW-BUDGET: A feature film produced for significantly less money than a Hollywood studio film.

MINIMUM: The lowest fee a writer may receive under the Writers Guild Minimum Basic Agreement.

MONTAGE: A series of short scenes that occurs over a period of hours, days, months, or years.

MOTIVATION: The driving force that prompts a character to react in a specific way.

MOW: The abbreviation for "movie of the week," which is a feature-length film made specifically for television.

NEGATIVE PICK-UP: The deal between a producer and a distributor, who pays a fee for the right to distribute the film. The fee is usually paid to the producer upon delivery of the film's cut negative. Many films are either partially or fully financed in this manner.

NET: The percentage of the film's profits, which is determined after production costs, prints and advertising, and so on, are deducted. The term "creative accounting" is often used when defining this term.

NO-BUDGET: A film produced for significantly less money than a low-budget film. (Terms like "beg," "borrow," "steal," and "max out one's credit cards" are associated with this definition.)

NONTHEATRICAL: A film that is not distributed in theaters but in other venues, such as television, videos, DVDs cable, schools, and libraries.

OBSTACLE: The hurdle a character must overcome to achieve his or her goal.

OFF CAMERA (OC): A sound or an action that is heard but not seen on film. Generally used only in television scripts.

OFF SCREEN (OS): A sound or an action that is heard but is not seen on film.

ON CAMERA: An actor or object that is seen by the camera.

ON THE NOSE: An expression describing dialogue that too obviously reveals a character's thoughts or feelings.

OPTION: The fee a writer is paid for the exclusive rights to his or her script for a specified period of time.

ORIGINAL SCREENPLAY: A screenplay that is not adapted from another source, such as a novel or play.

OVER THE TOP: An expression describing an action or scene that is extremely unbelievable or implausible.

PACING: A term referring to the rhythm and timing of the dialogue or action in each scene or throughout the entire script.

PACKAGE: The various elements and/or talent that agents or producers bring together to sell a project. The more talent the agent/agency packages in-house, the higher their total fee will be.

PASS: Term used when a story analyst, an agent, or a producer rejects material.

PAY OR PLAY: A contractual term meaning that an employer (for example, a producer) must pay the employee (for example, talent) regardless of whether services are performed.

PAYOFF: The result of specific actions or information that was set up early in the film.

PLAYER: A person well known in the industry for making high-profile deals.

PLOT: The events that drive a story forward toward its conclusion.

PLOT POINT: An important turning point in the events of a story.

POINTS: The percentage of net or gross profits of a film. Talent (writers, actors, directors, producers) may negotiate as part of their contract to receive points in addition to or instead of their fee. Gross points are the most beneficial.

POLISH: A term describing a minor rewrite; generally the final draft in the writing process. (This can entail dialogue, character, and/or action refinement.)

POSTPRODUCTION: Processes that occur after a film is shot. These include editing, looping, music scoring, opticals, and mixing.

POV: An abbreviation of the term "point of view," which is the perspective seen from the camera or a specific character in a screenplay or film.

PREMISE: The basic idea of the script's story.

PREPRODUCTION: The preparation for the filming of a script. This includes fine-tuning the script, hiring the cast and crew, preparing a script breakdown and budget, set construction, costume design, and location scouting.

PRINCIPAL PHOTOGRAPHY: The commencement of filming of the completed script.

PRINCIPAL PLAYERS: The main actors in the film.

PRODUCER: A person who finds material, develops scripts, hires talent, raises financing, and/or oversees the production of a film.

PRODUCTION ASSISTANT: A person who works in an entry-level position on a film production crew.

PRODUCTION COMPANY: The entity responsible for the development and production of a film.

PROFITS: The net and/or gross profits of a film.

PROJECTION: Producers or industry professionals' forecast of the potential earnings of a film. These projections are often covered in the trades.

PROPERTY: A term used to describe a script or other literary material.

PROTAGONIST: The main character or hero whose goals and actions drive the story forward.

PUBLIC DOMAIN: Material or property (such as a novel) available for the public's use without a fee because the copyright has expired or was not necessary.

RELEASE FORM: A legal document that protects a studio or a production company from charges of plagiarism or theft.

REMAKE: A new film based on an existing film.

RIGHT OF FIRST REFUSAL: Term used to describe the legal right a company has to accept or decline a property.

RISING ACTION: Terminology describing events that build upon one another with increasing momentum.

SCALE: The minimum WGA payment based on the film's budget status (low, medium, or high).

SCENE HEADING: In screenplay formatting, a term describing the location (EXT. HOUSE) and time (DAY) of the scene. Also known as a "slug line."

SCREENPLAY BY: The credit given to the writer or writers of a screenplay.
SECONDARY CHARACTER: A screenwriting term that also means "minor character."
SELL THROUGH: A film that is produced specifically to be released for sale, but not rental, to the home video and DVD market.
SETUP: (1) A term describing a specific action or information that will be paid off later in the script. For example: Your protagonist discovers a gold key in a secret trunk. (The setup.) This discovery needs to have a payoff. (2) A camera position from which a scene is filmed.
SEQUEL: A film that is a follow-up to an existing film. (Examples: *Rocky II, Grumpier Old Men, Spy Kids 2: Island of Lost Dreams, Meet the Fockers*.)
SEQUENCE: A group of scenes generally connected by a specific event in the screenplay.
SHARED CARD: An on-screen credit where more than one talent's name appears.
SHOOTING SCRIPT: The final draft of a screenplay; the one that will be filmed and includes the director's camera angles, scene numbers, and notes.
SINGLE CARD: An on-screen credit where the name of only one talent appears.
SLUG LINE: In screenplay formatting, a term describing the location (EXT. HOUSE) and time (DAY) of the scene. Also known as a "scene heading."
SOLICITED: A script submitted by an agent.
SPEC: A screenplay written on speculation (no payment) with the goal of selling, or a screenplay written before a deal is negotiated.

SPINE: Terminology used to describe the critical events in a story.

STABLE: An agent or agency's roster of clients.

STAGED READING: The live performance of a screenplay by actors.

STORY EDITOR: A person who supervises story analysts, reviews their coverage, and forwards promising material to their superiors.

STORYBOARD: A series of drawings placed in sequential order to illustrate the progression of shots in a film. Generally, only action or special-effects sequences are storyboarded since they are difficult and/or expensive to shoot.

STUDIO: A production company that develops, produces, and distributes major motion pictures and network television shows.

SUBPLOT: The secondary events in a story that are integrated with and further explore the main story line.

SUPER: A term in screenplay formatting used to describe the words superimposed over a scene. Generally used to identify the location and/or time period.

TAKE A MEETING: A slang expression meaning "to have a meeting." Another common colloquialism with a similar meaning is "do lunch."

THREE-ACT STRUCTURE: The structure commonly used in traditional narrative films. Act 1: sets up and establishes the story and characters; Act 2: conflicts and obstacles build; Act 3: climax and resolution.

THROUGH LINE: A term used to describe the main story line from beginning to end.

TITLES: The printed words at the beginning and end of a film. The film's title is known as the "main title."

TONE: A term describing the feeling or mood of the plot.

TOO MUCH BLACK: An expression meaning there is too much description and/or dialogue on a script page.

TRACK: A term describing the following of a project's progress.

TRADES/TRADE PAPERS: Daily and weekly newspapers or magazines that specialize in the news of the entertainment industry, e.g., *The Hollywood Reporter* and *Variety*.

TRAILER: A synopsized version of a film; a few minutes long, it is used to entice an audience to see the entire film.

TREATMENT: The prose version of a screenplay.

TURNAROUND: A script that is no longer in active development at a studio and is offered for sale to other studios or entities.

TWIST: A term describing an unexpected turning point in the story.

UNSOLICITED: A script that is submitted to a company without agent or manager representation.

VEHICLE: A term used to describe a script that offers an actor a breakthrough role.

VOICE-OVER: The narration heard off-screen and over what is seen on film. It can describe the past history of the character(s), the story, and/or the setting.

WRITTEN BY: The credit given to the writer of an original script that is based on his or her original story.

WORK-FOR-HIRE: Opposite of a spec script. A screenplay and/or treatment that a screenwriter has been paid to write. Generally, the rights of this work will be owned by the producer/company.

WRYLIES: In screenplays, the parenthetical descriptions that go underneath the character heading and before the character's dialogue: used to indicate emotion, tone, volume, to whom a character is speaking if otherwise unclear, or to clarify ambiguous subtext.

APPENDIX

CINEFILE—PRINT AND ONLINE RESOURCES

The following resources are listings, not endorsements. Parenthetical descriptions of resources are a *brief* overview, and most offer additional services. Due to companies' frequent address and phone number changes, only their Web sites are listed below.

TRADE PUBLICATIONS

Absolute Write: www.absolutewrite.com (online publication lists industry articles, agent listings, links, competitions, and message boards)
Authorlink: www.authorlink.com (online publication lists industry articles and agents)
Bigscreenbiz.com: bigscreenbiz.com (online publication lists links and directories)
***Creative Screenwriting*:** www.creativescreenwriting.com (industry articles, links, and contest information)
***Done Deal*:** www.scriptsales.com (online publication and newsletter resource for screenplay, pitch, treatment, and book

sales in the film industry; agency, attorney, and production company listings; industry articles; and contests)

Exposure: www.exposure.co.uk (online resource for low-budget independent filmmaking)

***Fade In* magazine:** www.fadeinmag.com (lists script competitions, industry articles, and links)

***Film Comment* magazine:** www.filmlinc.com (this is the Film Society of Lincoln Center's Web site: click on *Film Comment* icon; industry articles)

Film Threat: www.filmthreat.com (industry articles)

***Filmmaker Magazine*:** www.filmmakermagazine.com (industry articles; lists script competitions, events, and resources)

Filmmaking.net: www.filmmaking.net (online publication lists links, message boards, and industry articles)

FilmStew.com: www.filmstew.com (online publication: industry articles, resources, and subscription film-tracking service)

HollywoodLitSales.com: www.hollywoodlistsales.com (online publication: industry articles, resources, links, contests, and message boards)

***The Hollywood Reporter*:** www.hollywoodreporter.com (industry articles)

***Hollywood Scriptwriter*:** www.hollywoodscriptwriter.com (industry articles)

***The Independent*:** www.aivf.org (this is the Association of Video and Filmmakers' Web site: click on *The Independent* icon; lists competitions, seminars, resources and opportunities, links, and industry articles)

IndieClub.com: www.indieclub.com (online publication lists film festivals, networking, and industry articles)

Indiefilmpage: www.indiefilmpage.com (online publication lists film festivals, networking, and industry articles)

indieWIRE: www.indiewire.com (online publication: industry articles)

Inside Film Magazine Online: www.insidefilm.com (lists conferences, script competitions, and industry articles)

***Movie Magazine International*:** www.shoestring.org (this is the Shoestring Radio Theater's Web site: click on Movie Magazine International icon; radio program archives: interviews with talent, and more)

Moviebytes: www.moviebytes.com (online publication lists screenwriting competitions, contest report cards, resources, links, industry articles, and a subscription service: Who's Buying What)

***MovieMaker Magazine*:** www.moviemaker.com (available online and on newsstands: industry articles, links, jobs, and festivals)

NewEnglandFilm.com: www.newenglandfilm.com (online publication lists screenplay competitions, resources, events, links, and industry articles)

***Premiere Magazine*:** www.premieremag.com (industry articles)

Screentalk: wwwscreentalk.biz (online international screenwriting publication: industry articles, resources, and published scripts)

Screenwriter's Online Insider Report: www.screenwriter.com (this is the Screenwriters Online's Web site: click on Insider Report icon; industry articles, links, and resources)

Screenwriter's Utopia: www.screenwritersutopia.com (online screenwriting magazine lists competitions, seminars, and industry articles)

***Scr(i)pt* magazine:** www.scriptmag.com (industry articles, links, screenwriting contests, and resources)

Shooting People: www.shootingpeople.org (online U.K. and N.Y. publication: industry articles, networking, links, and resources)

UGO Screenwriter's Voice: www.screenwriting.ugo.com (online screenwriting publication lists competitions, seminars, links, and industry articles)

Underground Online: www.ugo.com (online publication lists resources, contests, and industry articles)

***Variety*:** www.ugo.com (daily, weekly, and online version: industry articles)

When Teens Write: www.teenswriters.net (online publication lists industry articles and resources)

Wordplay: www.wordplayer.com (online screenwriting publication: industry articles)

***Writer's Digest*:** www.writersdigest.com (lists script competitions, seminars, industry articles, and links)

Written By: www.wga.org/writtenby/writtenby.aspx (monthly publication of the WGA West: industry articles)

ORGANIZATIONS

Academy of Motion Picture Arts & Sciences: (Beverly Hills) www.oscars.org (sponsors the Academy Awards, educational programs, seminars, and Nicholl fellowships)

Academy of Television Arts & Sciences: (North Hollywood) www.emmys.org (education programs)

American Film Institute: (Los Angeles) www.afi.com (school and seminars)

American Screenwriters Association: (Cincinnati-based) www.asascreenwriters.com (nationwide chapters and affiliates: newsletter, conferences, resources, and competitions)

Association of Independent Video and Filmmakers: (New York City–based) www.aivf.org (workshops, publications, resources, facilities, and regional salons)

Cinestory: (Chicago-based) www.cinestory.com (sponsors Cinestory Screenwriting Awards, workshops, and seminars)

Directors Guild of America East and Directors Guild of America West: (New York City and Los Angeles) www.dga.org (publishes *DGA Magazine*: industry articles and online membership directory)

Dramatists Guild of America: (New York City–based) www.dramaguild.com (seminars)

Film Arts Foundation: (New York City–based) www.filmarts.org (seminars, screenings, and resources for independent filmmakers)

Film Independent: (Los Angeles–based) www.filmindependent.org (produces the Independent Spirit Awards and the Los Angeles Film Festival; seminars, screenings, producer series, Filmmaker Labs, cameras and casting rooms rentals, resource library with sample budgets and business plans, and other resources)

Filmmakers Collaborative: (New York City–based) www.filmmakers.org (facilities for independent filmmakers, seminars, and resources)

Film/Video Arts: (New York City–based) www.fva.com (equipment rental, seminars, and workshops)

The Foundation Center: (locations in New York City, Atlanta, Cleveland, San Francisco, and Washington, D.C.) www.fdncenter.org (resource center and online information for grants and workshops)

Grub Street: (Boston-based) www.grubstreet.org (seminars and workshops)

Independent Feature Project: (New York City–based) www.ifp.org (sponsors the Independent Feature Film Market, seminars, screenings, and other resources; check their Web site for additional nationwide chapters)

New York Women in Film and Television: (New York City–based) www.nywift.org (seminars and screenings)

Northwest Screenwriters Guild: (Seattle-based) www.nwsg.org (workshops, readings, and events)

The Organization of Black Screenwriters, Inc.: (Los Angeles–based) www.obswriter.com (script competitions, script development, agent outreach, and events)

Producers Guild of America: (Los Angeles–based) www.producersguild.org (resources and seminars)

Screen Actors Guild: (offices in New York City and Los Angeles) www.sag.org (resources and links)

The Sundance Institute: (Beverly Hills office) www.sundance.org (sponsors Sundance Film Festival, writers fellowship program, and events)

U.S. Copyright Office: (Washington, D.C.–based) www.copyright.gov (for application forms)

Volunteer Lawyers for the Arts: (nationwide locations) www.vlany.org (assists artists in need, and offers seminars)

Women in Film: (Hollywood-based; nationwide and international chapters) www.wif.org (seminars and screenings)

Women in Film & Video/New England: (Boston-based) www.wifvne.org (seminars and screenings)

Writers Guild of America, East: (New York City–based) www.wgaeast.org (writers' union, script registration, resources, seminars, links, and more)

Writers Guild of America, West: (Los Angeles–based) www.wga.org (writers' union, script registration, resources, seminars, links, and more. This site also provides extensive resources for researching information about your script, including Ask the Experts: organizations that provide free research information such as government departments, medical authorities, psychological references, and religious information

Writers Guild of Canada (WGC): www.writersguildofcanada.com (script registration, links, resources, and more)

MARKETING GUIDES

The following publications can be purchased through the Web sites listed below.

The Hollywood Creative Directory: www.hcdonline.com (lists studios, networks, production companies, and executives with phone, fax, addresses, selected produced credits, staff and titles)

The Hollywood Representation Directory: www.hcdonline.com (lists agents and managers nationwide)

Blu-Book Film Production Directory: www.hcdonline.com (lists contact information for TV, commercials and music video production)

WHERE TO BUY PUBLISHED SCREENPLAYS

Look under "Screenplays" on the Internet and you will find links to assist you in your search. Also, major bookstores carry published scripts.

Hollywood Book City: www.hollywoodbookcity.com
Script City: www.scriptcity.net
The Script Shack: www.scriptshack.com
Writers Store: www.writersstore.com (also free biweekly e-zines, featuring articles and writing tips)

WHERE TO DOWNLOAD FREE PUBLISHED SCREENPLAYS

The Daily Script: www.dailyscript.com
Drew's Script-O-Rama: www.script-o-rama.com
iScriptdb: www.iscriptdb.com
ScriptCrawler: www.scriptcrawler.net
Simply Scripts: www.simplyscripts.com
Twiz TV: www.twiztv.com/scripts
UGO Movie-Page.com: www.movie-page.com/movie_scripts.htm

ADDITIONAL RESOURCES

Contact your state arts council and local film commissions for grants and other opportunities.

filmtracker.com: www.filmtracker.com (database of films in development)

IMDbPro.com: www.imdbpro.com (representation listings, company directory, and production charts)
IndieFilms: www.indiefilms.com (Hollywood-based network that helps independent filmmakers find investors, grants, funds, and distributors for their features, shorts, and documentaries)
The Internet Movie Database: www.imdb.com (online publication: information on thousands of films, biographies of actors, and directors)
Mandy's Film and TV Production Directory: www.mandy.com (online resource and directory)
MoviePartners.com: www.moviepartners.com (resources, industry links, and online directory of talent and who represents them)
whoRepresents.com: www.whorepresents.com (online directory of talent and who represents them)

If you live in the United Kingdom and are researching agents and other helpful links, visit: *www.author-network.com/agents.html.*

If you live in Australia or New Zealand and are researching agents and other helpful links, visit: *home.vicnet.net.au/~ozlit/agents.html.*

If you live in Canada, visit The Canadian Authors Association for helpful links at: *www.canauthors.org/pubs.html.*

If you live outside of the United States, the International Affiliation of Writers Guilds (IAWG), an international body representing guilds of professional screenwriters, has guilds in the countries listed below.

Australian Writers' Guild: www.awg.com.au

Irish Playwrights and Screenwriters' Guild: www.script.ie
New Zealand Writers Guild: www.nzwritersguild.org.nz
Société des auteurs de radio, télévision et cinéma (SARTEC): www.sartec.qc.ca (French-language Canada)
Writers Guild of Great Britain: www.writersguild.org.uk

ABOUT THE AUTHOR

Susan Kouguell is chairperson of Su-City Pictures East, a motion picture consulting company founded in 1990. More than one thousand international clients include writers, filmmakers, agents, and production companies, as well as the major studios, including Miramax, Warner Bros., and Fine Line Features. Su-City screenwriting clients won or were finalists at many competitions including: Nicholls, Sundance Labs, Chesterfield, American Screenwriters Association, Nantucket, Austin, Writer's Network, New York Drama League, and Beigel. Filmmaking clients won or were the official selection at many international festivals, including: London International, South by Southwest, and the Los Angeles Independent Film Festival. Awards include: Kevin Bacon's *Losing Chase* (Golden Globe Best Actress: Helen Mirren; Globe Nominee: Beau Bridges); Tag Purvis's *Red Dirt* (Slam Dunk: Best Actors Karen Black/Walton Goggins; Chicago Gay & Lesbian Fest: Best Dramatic Feature; Beverly Hills International: Best Director); Jay Chandrasekhar's *Puddle Cruiser* (Hamptons Grand Prize; Sundance Official Selection); Jane Spencer's *Little Noises* (Sundance Grand Jury nominee); and

Joe Berlinger and Bruce Sinofsky's *Brother's Keeper* (Sundance Audience Award/Grand Jury nominee).

Kouguell cowrote with Carl Capotorto *The Suicide Club* (Anjelica Films), wrote voice-over narrations for *Murder One* and *Dakota* (Miramax), and over a dozen features for independent production companies. A two-time finalist for the Sundance Screenwriters Laboratory, she received fifteen screenwriting and film production grants and fellowships from the Jerome Foundation, the MacDowell Colony, the New York Foundation for the Arts, the Edward Albee Foundation, and others. Six of her short internationally award-winning films (made in collaboration with Ernest Marrero) are in the archives and permanent collection of the Museum of Modern Art and were included in the Whitney Museum of American Art Biennial. Kouguell worked with director Louis Malle on the documentary *And the Pursuit of Happiness,* and she was the screenplay doctor and associate producer of the features *Rum & Coke,* directed by Maria Escobedo, and Jay Craven's *Where the Rivers Flow North*.

Kouguell teaches screenwriting, film, and business of writing courses at Tufts University, Purchase College, and Screenwriters Online. She has presented numerous film industry seminars to organizations and universities, including the Writers Guild of America the Directors Guild of America, Screenwriting Expo, *Scr(i)pt* magazine's PitchFest, Independent Feature Project, Independent Feature Film Market, New York Women in Film & Television, Women in Film/Video New England, Atlantic Film & Video Producers Conference in Canada, New England Screenwriters Conference, New York University, Temple University, The New School, and Emerson and Hunter colleges. Kouguell is a regular contributor to many screenwriting and film publications.

INDEX